STEADFAST PARENTS
Study Guide

STEADFAST PARENTS

Strategies to Help Your Children
Run the Race of Life *and Win*

Based on the movie *Steadfast*

Barbara Shoner

Novel Idea Press

The feature film, *Steadfast*, can be viewed on
Amazon Prime Video at

or visit our website at www.steadfastthemovie.com.

CONTENTS

Your life might be the only Bible someone else reads.
When actions speak louder than words,
will they be enough to save someone?

Introduction

Therefore, since we are surrounded by such a great cloud of witnesses, let us throw off everything that hinders and the sin that so easily entangles. And let us run with perserverance the race marked out for us, fixing our eyes on Jesus, the pioneer and perfecter of faith. For the joy set before him he endured the cross, scorning its shame, and sat down at the right hand of the throne of God. Consider him who endured such opposition from sinners, so that you will not grow weary and lose heart (Hebrews 12:1-3 NIV).

The Starting Line

Let us run with endurance the race set before us...
Hebrews 12:1 TLV

In the Bible, Christian living is compared to running a race. This race, though, is not a sprint but a marathon. Getting to the finish line is a lifelong race of faith which takes steadfastness. Training is required to run a successful race. As the Apostle Paul explained:

> All athletes are disciplined in their training. They do it to win a prize that will fade away, but we do it for an eternal prize. So I run with purpose in every step. I am not just shadowboxing. I discipline my body like an athlete, training it to do what it should. Otherwise, I fear that after preaching to others I myself might be disqualified. (1 Corinthians 9:25-27 NLT)

To run victoriously, we must first get in shape. We need to spiritually train ourselves, and "remove from our lives anything that would slow us down and the sin that so often makes us fall" (Hebrews 12:1).

Next, it is important to determine our course and then stay on the right track so we don't get disqualified. God sets the race before us and

He determines where we are to run. He chooses each person's path according to His divine purpose. Some might have an easier road while others may find their route more difficult. But we aren't to stop in the middle of the race and question why our course might be different from someone else's. We are to just keep running so that "the good work God began in [us] will continue until he completes it on the day when Jesus Christ comes again" (Philippians 1:6).

While running our course there may be mountains to climb, muck to wade through, potholes to go around, and rocks to avoid, but we are to continue the race, "fixing our eyes on Jesus" (Hebrews 12:2 NIV). By making Jesus our focal point instead of looking at the spectators or the things that can so easily trip us up, we will continue to run and not quit. We may stumble or even fall, but we'll be able to finish the race. The Bible encourages us to "persevere so that when [we] have done the will of God, [we] will receive what he has promised" (Hebrews 10:36 NIV).

Since the race of faith is an endurance run and not a hundred yard dash, even though we can't see the finish line we must trust in God to guide us there. At times when it seems that we are straining to the breaking point, we need to keep in mind that our competition is not the other runners. It's satan, who will do anything to keep us from the finish line.

Motivation helps us endure to the end of the race. And what exactly is our motivation? To gain the prize. Paul summed it up this way: "Brothers and sisters, I know that I still have a long way to go. But there is one thing I do: I forget what is in the past and try as hard as I can to reach the goal before me. I keep running hard toward the finish line to get the prize that is mine because God has called me through Christ Jesus to life up there in heaven" (Philippians 3:13-14).

Steadfast Parents is designed to provide parents with training and endurance to help their children stay in the race. There are eight topics addressed in this study guide: bullying, purity, eating disorders, substance abuse, cutting, abuse (physical, emotional and sexual), suicide, and witnessing; however, there are nine actual lessons. Because bullying is such a broad issue, there are two lessons that deal with bullying. The first one discusses bullying in general, while the second lesson focuses on bystanders.

With each session there is a video clip from the movie to watch, as well as a clip of a testimony from someone who has personally dealt with that issue. Some lessons have more than one testimony. There is also an invitational prayer with each subject, in case you haven't fully committed your life to Christ. Scenes from the movie, the testimonies, and the songs for each session are available for free by accessing this link – https://drive.google.com/open?id=1PUKEj_qSLlTPF4PC3x6-zB_czZIu9 – and will enhance your learning experience.

Listening to a song from the soundtrack is a great way to end the session as you absorb the lesson and praise the Lord for what He is doing in your life and the lives of your children. Take the time to write down your thoughts to the questions posed. An answer key to the general questions is included at the end of this book. Also, share with your children the websites that are included on the resources page for each study, and please don't hesitate to seek professional help for them or you, if needed. Most importantly, remember Jesus is still the solution to every problem.

For Group Study

The outline for this study consists of: 1) Opening prayer (leaders may add their own prayer); 2) Discussion groups (Setting the Pace); 3) Watching a clip from the movie, *Steadfast*; 4) Lesson (Running the Race); 5) Watching a testimony from someone who has dealt with the issue; 6) Call to Jesus/invitation (Preparing for the Finish Line); 7) Worship with a song from the Steadfast soundtrack; and 8) Closing prayer (Endurance).

The progression of this study is flexible and each chapter is standalone so they can be shared in any order. Discussion may take place with everyone together as one group or separated into smaller, more intimate groups. The discussion period can be as extensive or limited as need be, depending on the available time frame. Simply pick and choose which questions to discuss if there isn't enough time for all of them.

To aid in preparation time, sample answers are provided at the end of this book for many of the discussion questions. The lesson portion of each study is about 15-20 minutes, while the movie clips, music, and testimony times vary. The songs range between one and half minutes to five minutes, and the movie clips and testimonies are a few minutes to around fifteen minutes. Some topics have more than one testimony. If time is limited, choose the one you feel your participants will connect with the most.

Discussion time is a great opportunity to learn more about the needs of each parent and what is going on with their children. Welcome participation by reminding everyone that anything shared in group is confidential. "What's said in group, stays in group." Encourage openness and respect. Ensure them that with many questions there are no right or wrong answers, but instead offers everyone an opportunity to share their feelings and experiences. Allow each person a chance to speak.

Reproducible worksheets for the discussion questions are available on our website. Please feel free to copy them for your use: www.steadfasthemovie.com/steadfast-study-guide-resources. The list of questions can be given to each person to fill out before or during discussion time, if desired. Otherwise, leaders can bypass this worksheet and instead introduce each question while discussing the matter orally. Additionally, a tips and resources handout is available at the end of each session (and on our website for copying) that not only highlights key points of the lesson, but also lists resources and helpline contact numbers. Encouraging scriptures and a memory verse are also included, as well as an invitational prayer to give readers an opportunity to come to the Lord on their own. May the Lord bless your group time and may there be a mighty move of the Holy Spirit for the changing of lives.

Bullying

BULLYING

Bible References Luke 6:29; John 18:19–23; 2 Timothy 1:7; Romans 12:17–21; Psalm 46:1; Hebrews 13:5; Philippians 4:13; Matthew 5:16, 7:12, 10:16; James 1:5; 1 Samuel

> **Memory Verse:** God is our protection and source of strength. He is always ready to help us in times of trouble (Psalm 46:1).

✝ Opening Prayer: Lord, grant me wisdom and give me peace as I read Your Word, Amen!

Watch BULLYING–LESSON Video Clip

SETTING THE PACE – Your Thoughts and Experiences/ Discussion Group

Bullying is described as *unwanted, aggressive behavior towards someone, often repeatedly*. Let's discuss what bullying means to you:

1. What are some examples of bullying?

2. Were you ever bullied as a child?

3. Were you ever a bully?

4. Have you ever witnessed someone being bullied?

5. What do you believe make some people targets for bullying?

6. Why do you believe some people become bullies?

Activities for Groups:

Break into smaller groups. Assign each group to brainstorm and come up with a bullying scenario to act out. Watch each group perform, then discuss what can be learned from the skits.

<u>Play Status Card</u>[1]:

Give everyone a playing card face down. They are not to look at the card. Everyone then places the card against their forehead facing out (another option is to tape the card to each person's forehead), or holds the card in their hand facing out, and walks around mingling with each other. Treat each other based on the value of each person's card: 2-6 are the lowest, no one pays much attention to them or wants to hang out with them. 7-10 are in the middle, average but not too cool. The J, Q, K, and Ace are the royal cards. They are the best, the most popular, and the ones everyone wants to hang around with. After a few minutes, have everyone get into the group that they feel they belong in based on how they were treated. Let them look at their card to see if they guessed right. Discuss how it felt to be treated that way. Then discuss Matthew 7:12, "Treat others as you want them to treat you" (the Golden Rule).

RUNNING THE RACE – Study

One of the greatest heartbreaks for any parent is to experience your child going through the torture of being bullied. It's no less heartbreaking to find out that your child is the perpetrator. Unfortunately, bullying is a growing trend that's causing devastating consequences. School shootings and countless suicides have been attributed to bullying. For instance, at a Cleveland high school, a teen described as an outcast who had apparently been bullied, opened fire in the cafeteria, killing one student and wounding four others.[1]

A seventh grader shot and killed a teacher and wounded two other students at his Nevada school. He'd evidently been bullied, and one witness said, "He was yelling a bunch of things while we were running. He was yelling stuff like, 'Why are you laughing at me? Why are you doing this to me?'" He then shot himself to death.[2]

A twelve-year-old Florida girl jumped to her death from atop an abandoned cement factory after being viciously cyberbullied,[3] while a

16

fifteen-year-old girl leaped off the roof of a 27-story apartment building after a petition to have her commit suicide was started online.[4]

Sadly, these are but a few of the tragic incidents that have happened nationwide due, in part, to bullying. Statistics show that over 3.2 million students are victims of bullying each year, approximately 160,000 teens skip school every day because of bullying, and 1 in 10 students drop out of school because of repeated bullying.[5]

School-age children act much differently than toddlers, who will cry out and tattle the instant someone is being mean to them. And the older kids get, the less willing they are to open up. You may not even be aware of the torment your child is going through. While your child may not verbalize it, however, there are some warning signs to watch out for:

- Edgy; angry—explodes easily
- Withdrawn
- Anxiety; moodiness
- Doesn't want to go to school; disinterested in school activities
- Clothing or other personal items are damaged or missing
- Unexplained injuries—cuts, scratches, bruises
- Fearful
- Difficulty eating and/or sleeping
- Physical symptoms—headaches, stomachaches, tired
- Getting involved with drugs and/or alcohol
- Loss of friends

Some of these symptoms can be normal for teenagers and don't indicate bullying, but that's where you must be intuitive and pray for the Holy Spirit to guide you in discerning what is really going on. It's important for your children to understand that it's safe to talk to you about things. Many are reluctant to talk to a parent because of fear over how the parent will react. Not only are they afraid that the parent will overreact, but they often are afraid of retaliation by the bully for snitching, and may also be embarrassed and ashamed. Allow them to gain some control by letting them help decide the best course of action, as long as it won't put your children in further danger. Take time to pray together and seek the Lord's wisdom on how to handle things.

God's Word gives us examples on how to manage these trials God's way. A scripture that often gets misconstrued by well-meaning parents is Luke 6:29: "If someone hits you on the side of your face, let them hit the other side too."

While some parents may advise their children to always back down, the Lord doesn't expect us to put ourselves in danger. This passage actually refers to an insult, not to physical harm. Turning the other cheek means not to return insult for insult in retaliation. We are not to be mean back, but Jesus doesn't expect us to not defend ourselves.

Therefore, if your children are victims of bullying, teach them that it's not right to seek revenge, but it is okay to stand up for ourselves. The perfect example of this comes from Jesus himself. When the guard of the High Priest slapped Jesus on the face, he didn't stand silently and wait for the guard to do it again. He defended himself with probing words: "If I said something wrong, tell everyone here what was wrong. But if what I said is right, then why do you hit me?" (John 18:19-23)

Jesus asked his attacker why he was wrongly treating him that way. In the same manner, we are not to hurt the bully back, but we are to defend ourselves wisely without anger. We should handle the situation in a way that won't cause further tension and allows us to escape safely. We are not to fear, but to be wise and use restraint "[f]or God did not give us a spirit of fear, but of power and love and self-control" (2 Timothy 1:7 NET).

God's Word tells us further in Romans 12:17-21 the appropriate way we should handle those who mistreat us:

> If someone does you wrong, don't try to pay them

back by hurting them. Try to do what everyone thinks is right. Do the best you can to live in peace with everyone. My friends, don't try to punish anyone who does wrong to you. Wait for God to punish them with his anger. In the Scriptures the Lord says,

"I am the one who punishes; I will pay people back." But you should do this: "If you have enemies who are hungry, give them something to eat. If you have enemies who are thirsty, give them something to drink. In doing this you will make them feel ashamed."

Don't let evil defeat you, but defeat evil by doing good.

Thus, teach your children that retaliation is not an option and they should do what they can to live at peace with others. However, while they are to leave revenge to God, they should still stand up for themselves and others, and report bullying to their parents and/or other trusted authority. Explain the difference between tattling (telling to get someone in trouble) and telling to keep someone safe.

Assure them that "God is our protection and source of strength. He is always ready to help us in times of trouble" (Psalm 46:1), and while you as a parent may not be able to physically be there when they are going through something, that the Lord is always there and your children can turn to God at any time. God's Word makes these very promises to us in Hebrews 13:5:

Since God assures us, "I'll never let you down, never walk off and leave you," we can boldly quote, God is there, ready to help; I'm fearless no matter what. Who or what can get to me?" (MSG)

We can be assured that God is on our side! While the Lord may not always remove us from every situation, He will always help us to deal with our problems and will use these trials to build our character. Philippians 4:13 says, "Christ is the one who gives me the strength I need to do whatever I must do."

Impart to your children that this strength will be different depending on the circumstances. They will need to assess each situation to decide when it's appropriate to back down and when they need to take a stand. Bullies like to dominate their victims and will often pick on those who won't defend themselves. Therefore, as long as the situation won't become more dangerous by doing so, we should ask the Lord to help us to respond like Jesus did. Acting confident may be enough to cause the bully to back down.

Other guidelines to share with your children to prevent bullying include:

- Avoid being alone
- Stay away from places where bullies hang out
- Keep calm
- Ignore a bully if possible
- Stay near adults—most bullying does not happen when adults are around
- Be self-confident—body language can express this: stand straight, head up, and don't avoid making eye contact

When it comes to cyber-bullying, children may be even more reluctant to tell a parent for fear that their computers, phones and other electronics will be taken away. While this seems like the logical way to keep our children safe, instead it makes our children feel like they're being punished. To prevent them from feeling even more victimized, instead change passwords, phone numbers, block the perpetrators, keep records of the messages, and report the cyberbullying.

In Matthew 10:16, Jesus warns us about troubles and tells us how we should act: "Listen! I am sending you, and you will be like sheep among wolves. So be smart like snakes. But also be like doves and don't hurt anyone." Impart to your children that when they need to be smart but don't really know how to handle something, the Bible advises: "Do any of you need wisdom? Ask God for it. He is generous and enjoys giving to everyone. So He will give wisdom" (James 1:5). Teach your children that the Lord will give wisdom to all who seek it.

When this wisdom leads your kids to run from a situation, reassure them that they shouldn't be ashamed to do so and that doesn't make them cowards. While David didn't back down from Goliath, years later when King Saul decided to kill David, the same man who stood up to a giant fled from the King (1 Samuel). There are times when wisdom will tell them to flee, but that doesn't mean they're weak. That just means they are listening to and trusting in God to help them determine what actions to take in each given situation.

But what if your children are the perpetrators? Bullies suffer as well as the victims, so it's important to take action. They may endure depression, struggle academically and with jobs, get involved with gangs and drugs, and often will become even more aggressive in adulthood, which can lead to abusive relationships. Here are some warning signs to be aware of when determining whether your child may be a bully:

- Fits of rage; easily loses temper
- Lack of empathy for others
- Dominates his or her peers
- Overly confident/cocky
- Physically larger and stronger than peers
- Hates to lose
- Blames others for everything
- Enjoys power and control
- Derives pleasure from other's pain
- Impulsive
- Gang activity; vandalism; increased use of drugs and/or alcohol
- Lacks social skills

- Defiant
- Tests authority
- Problems at school/home

As with victim status, having some of these traits doesn't mean that your children are or will be bullies. Again, pray to be made aware if this is truly the case with your kids. However, if there is evidence of bullying, then steps should be taken. Your children need to be made aware that this type of behavior will not be tolerated. Make sure no bullying is going on in the family dynamics, give clear consequences, and teach your children about having compassion for others. Instill in them the Golden Rule found in Matthew 7:12: "Treat others as you want them to treat you." Seek professional help if needed.

While it may be despairing to deal with children who are bullies, remember how God shows mercy and grace to even the worst of sinners, and that God has the power to change them.

As parents we should impart to our children that above all, they should handle themselves in a way that is a good example to others and brings glory to God. The Bible says, "In the same way, you should be a light for other people. Live so that they will see the good things you do and praise your Father in heaven" (Matthew 5:16).

In the movie, Steadfast, Jesse is relentlessly bullied. His main antagonist is Brady. While driving drunk one night, Brady's brother causes an auto accident that kills Jesse's mother. Instead of facing what his brother had done, Brady takes his anger out on Jesse for Brady's brother being in jail. He uses his misplaced resentment to continually harass Jesse. Not only does Jesse have to deal with the bullying, but also with the loss of his mother and of his father, who uses his own grief to become a workaholic and completely ignore Jesse.

Coming from a non-Christian home, Jesse doesn't know the love and grace that's found in Christ. When he becomes overwhelmed, Jesse has no hope to get him through the trials. He feels all alone in his pain and doesn't have the strength to persevere.

Moriah, on the other hand, has faith and a relationship with her heavenly Father. She is constantly teased by a jealous Claire. There are times when Moriah breaks down, but she still continues to act in the right way. She defeats evil by doing good. Moriah has hope and the strength of the Lord to guide her, and her actions become a testimony to Claire who knows nothing about God but wants what Moriah has. Moriah is able to handle her bullying in a way that glorifies God and helps someone else.

So, how will your children handle things? Will they feel hopeless or will they be filled with the peace that only comes through knowing Christ? Whether our children are victims or bullies, it's important for us to instill in them that they are children of the Most High God. Victims are not defined by what a bully might say or do to them. They are who God says they are! The Lord created us in His image and we are beautiful to Him.

Likewise, Jesus will forgive even the worst of bullies. "'For I know the plans I have for you,' declares the Lord. 'Plans to prosper you and not to harm you, plans to give you hope and a future'" (Jeremiah 29:11).

By not being victims ourselves to ignorance or indifference when it comes to what is going on in our children's lives, and by advocating for our children, we can help them to be steadfast in whatever comes their way.

Watch TESTIMONY–BULLYING Video Clip

PREPARING FOR THE FINISH LINE – Invitation

If you have been beat up and beat down way too long and don't know what to do anymore—if you need the strength to deal with situations in your children's lives, and want to have the hope, peace, protection, and wisdom that can only come from the Lord Jesus Christ, please repeat this prayer:

Lord Jesus, I ask you to come into my life and forgive me for all of my sins. I believe in my heart and confess with my mouth that You died for my sins but rose on the third day so that I might be saved.[6] With You I never have to go through life alone, and I am an overcomer! Thank You, Jesus, for Your gift of eternal life. In Your precious name I pray, Amen!

🎵 WORSHIP – Listen to the Song *LET IT GO*

👟 ENDURANCE – Closing Prayer

Heavenly Father, please protect my children from bullying. If my children are victims, Lord, please give them wisdom, peace, and safety, and let them know they are not alone—that You are always with them. If my children are bullies, Lord, please give them compassion for others. Fill them with Your love so they don't have to build themselves up by beating others down. And if my children become witnesses to bullying, Lord, please give them the courage to stand up for what is right. For me as a parent, Lord, guide me in how I should handle each situation and give me favor with my children. Thank You that through You we are more than conquerors! In Jesus' name I pray, Amen!

TIPS AND RESOURCES FOR YOUR CHILDREN – BULLYING

Memory Verse: God is our protection and source of strength. He is always ready to help us in times of trouble (Psalm 46:1).

Ways to prevent bullying:

1. Pray to the Lord for help.
2. Act confident.
3. Diffuse with humor if possible.
4. Avoid being alone.
5. Stay away from places where bullies hang out.
6. Remain calm.
7. Keep near adults.
8. If in danger, don't be ashamed to run.
9. Talk about it with a parent, pastor, school counselor, or someone else you trust.
10. Never buy into anything that bullies say about you or do to you. *You are a wonderfully made child of the One True King.*

Ways to deal with cyberbullying:

1. Be careful of what you post and who you "friend."
2. Block bullies from your social media and phone.
3. Report cyberbullying to the internet service provider, the website, and/or cell phone company.
4. Contact police if threats of harm are made.

Help Lines:

1-877-332-7333   Real Help for Teens Hotline
1-800-273-8255   24/7 Crisis Call Center
1-800-420-1479   CyberBullying Hotline—call or text
1-866-444-6996   Anti-Bullying Hotline
1-800-273-TALK   National Suicide Prevention Hotline

Links:

www.stopbullying.gov

www.bullying.org

http://www.stompoutbullying.org/livechat_portal.php

Sword of the Spirit:

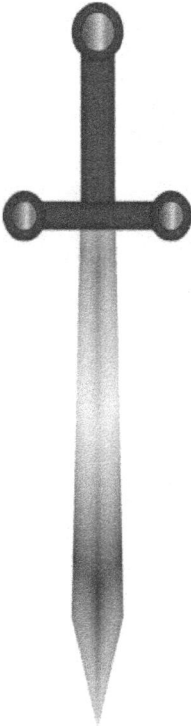

For God did not give us a spirit of fear, but of power and love and self-control (2 Timothy 1:7 NET).

So be strong and courageous! Do not be afraid and do not panic before them. For the Lord your God will personally go ahead of you. He will neither fail you nor abandon you (Deut. 31:6 NLT).

You, Lord, are the light that keeps me safe. I am not afraid of anyone. You protect me, and I have no fears (Psalm 27:1 CEV).

You shall not take vengeance, nor bear any grudge against the sons of your people, but you shall love your neighbor as yourself; I am the Lord (Leviticus 19:18 NASB).

Don't let evil defeat you, but defeat evil by doing good (Romans 12:21).

Bullying and the Bystander

BULLYING AND THE BYSTANDER

Bible References Luke 10:25–37, 19:1–10; John 8:1–11, 13:34, 15:13; Genesis 50:20; Deuteronomy 6:18; Romans 10:9

Memory Verse: Do what is right and good in the Lord's sight so that it may go well with you (Deut. 6:18 NIV).

✝ **Opening Prayer:** Lord, strengthen me with Your Word and fill me with compassion, Amen!

Watch BULLYING/BYSTANDER–LESSON Video Clip

SETTING THE PACE – Your Thoughts/Discussion Group Discussion Group

What would you do if:

1. Your child is afraid to go to school because a bully constantly pushes him/her around.

2. Your daughter texts her friend about a guy she thinks is hot. Her "friend" sends her texts to a bunch of other people, including the guy.

3. A group of students tease your child for either his/her outfit/hair/height/voice/glasses/being overweight.

4. Your child reads an untrue post or blog that says he or she has had sex with a classmate.

5. Someone puts up flyers or posts altered pictures of your child.

6. Your child is purposefully excluded from participating with others (lunch, a sport, etc.).

7. Your child gets threatening texts.

8. A bully starts cruelly imitating your child.

9. Someone is spreading nasty rumors about your child.

10. Your child's best friend starts ignoring him/her.

11. Your child finds out that he/she wasn't invited to a party that everyone else is going to.

12. Someone constantly posts mean comments to your child's status.

RUNNING THE RACE – Study

After she posted 144 times on Twitter about being abused and no one reached out, the eighteen-year-old girl killed herself.[1] A homeless man lay dying on the street while people walked around him and even took pictures.[2] Twenty people saw ten men and boys gang rape and beat a fifteen-year-old girl on a high school campus and no one helped or even contacted the authorities.[3] Albert Einstein said, "The world is too dangerous to live in, not because of the people who do evil, but because of the people who sit and let it happen."

As parents we must convey to our children the importance of standing up for other people. Bullies like an audience and while bullying rarely takes place in front of adults, it frequently happens in front of peers. Bullies could often be discouraged if bystanders would show disapproval or step in.

Unfortunately, a study reports that while bullying takes place in front of other kids 86 percent of the time, only 20 percent of witnesses ever intervene.[4] When other youth don't do anything to stop it, they are essentially encouraging the bullies. They're giving bullies the message that it's okay to do what they are doing.

Why do so many stand by while others are being mistreated? Six of the most frequently cited reasons that young people give for why they choose not to intervene to stop bullying are:

1. **"Someone else will surely step in."** This is the belief that an adult or someone else will stop it. However, most bullying doesn't take place with adults present and while everyone else is assuming others will take responsibility, no one ends up helping.

2. **"If I say anything, he'll turn on me next!"** That shouldn't stop us from trying to help the victim. It's up to us to use wisdom to either say something directly to the bully or go to an authority figure for help.

3. **"I don't like what the bully is doing, but she is still my friend."** Conflict is a part of life and this may be where children need to learn to handle disagreements by challenging their friend's actions. Also, they may wish to consider whether they really want to be friends with someone who treats others so cruelly.

4. **"I would say something, but the victim and I aren't really friends."** Just because we may not know the person being bullied, does that excuse us from the responsibility? No one deserves to be mistreated.

5. **"You're asking me to stand out on purpose?"** Most of us just want to blend in, but we are called to stand up for the abused.

6. **"I just don't know what to do to make it stop."** Each situation is different, so it's important to have a game plan. Each person should pray for the courage to speak up when circumstances call for it or the wisdom to know who to go to for help when an authority figure is needed.[5]

In Luke 10:25-37, Jesus says to "love your neighbor the same as you love yourself," and He illustrates how we should act in a bystander situation. This is where we get the expression "Good Samaritan." The story involves a man who was beaten and left for dead on the side of the road. A priest comes down that same road, but when he sees the man, he ignores him. A Levite approaches but when he notices the hurt man, he crosses the street to avoid him. Finally, a Samaritan traveling down the road feels sorry for the man, cleans his wounds and takes him to get help. Jesus tells us that we are to act in the same manner as the Samaritan.

It takes a lot of courage to intervene, but we must stand up for what is right. This standard applies to us as adults as well as for our children. Even when no one else is doing anything about it, that doesn't mean it's okay. Communicate to your children that if they witness someone being bullied, obviously they should never join in, but they also shouldn't just stand there. A bully will perceive that as encouragement. Sometimes all it may take to end an incident is to defend the person being bullied. This might shock or embarrass the bully into stopping.

However, your children shouldn't step in if it means putting themselves in danger. That's when they should seek an authority figure for help, and ask to remain anonymous if there's a fear of retaliation. Further, as the Good Samaritan nursed the man back to health, they too should reach out to the victim after the incident to see if they can help that person in any way.

There's another story in the Bible that tells of a time when Jesus stood up to others and defended someone. In John 8:1-11, a group of Pharisees brought a woman before Jesus who had been caught in the act of adultery. They asked Jesus if they should stone her as the law commanded. Jesus used wise words to disband the bullies. After telling them that whoever has never sinned should throw the first stone, they all dropped their rocks and walked away, leaving the victim alone.

Jesus reveals two points in this story. Though the woman was a victim of bullying, as an adulteress she had sinned. Jesus not only stood up to the bullies for her, but He also gave mercy to her as a sinner.

This is likewise true in the story of Zaccheus, told in Luke 19:1-10. Zaccheus was a hated tax collector. He had sinned by extorting money from the people. When Jesus visited Jericho, Zaccheus was determined to see him. However, whether it was because Zaccheus was short or whether the townspeople who hated him were purposely keeping him from seeing, Zaccheus resorted to climbing a sycamore tree in order to catch a glimpse of Jesus. Jesus had no trouble spotting Zaccheus though, and He invited Himself to dine at Zacchaeus' house, much to the resentment of the crowd. Zacchaeus, the victim, was led away from the angry mob by Jesus; Zacchaeus, the bully, found grace in the forgiveness of Jesus, and in turn, repented by giving half of his possessions to the poor and paying back four times the amount to anyone he had ever cheated.

Like Jesus, we are also to be advocates and show compassion to victims and forgiveness to bullies. Our actions may be what turns a situation or someone's life around. For those who are bullies, as parents we should teach them to embrace a motto from Abraham Lincoln: "I would rather be a little nobody than an evil somebody." Teach forgiveness to those who are victims, using as an example what Joseph forgivingly said to his brothers after they had plotted to kill him: "You tried to harm me, but God made it turn out for the best" (Genesis 50:20 CEV). And for those who are bystanders, there's a saying: "If you stand for nothing, you will fall for anything." Deuteronomy 6:18 reminds us to "[d]o what is right and good in the LORD's sight" (NIV).

We are called take a stand! Reverend Theodore Hesburgh said, "My basic principle is that you don't make decisions because they are easy; you don't make them because they're popular; you make them because they're right." Let's remind our children that the Lord has a plan and a purpose for all of our lives and we are to do what is right, and trust Him to have our backs.

 Watch TESTIMONY–BULLYING/BYSTANDERS Video Clip

 PREPARING FOR THE FINISH LINE – Invitation

If you have found yourself stuck in the middle and sitting on the fence far too long, today is the day to stand up for Jesus. Invite Him now to take an active role in your life by repeating this prayer:

Jesus, I am tired of being on the sidelines and I now want to be a part of the winning team. I ask You to take over and to cleanse me from all of my sins. I believe in my heart and confess with my mouth that You laid down Your life for me so that I might be saved.[6] *Thank You, Jesus, that I am no longer an onlooker but a part of the body of believers. In Your precious name I pray, Amen!*

🎵 WORSHIP – Listen to the Song *DESPERATE*

👟 ENDURANCE – Closing Prayer

Lord, I thank You that even though we live in an unjust world, we have a just God. And as You made the ultimate sacrifice of dying on the cross to save us from our sins, I ask that my children and I have that same commitment to our fellow man. Give me the courage to live out Your commandment that tells us to love one another the way that You have loved us[7] so that I can be a role model for my children to follow. Give my children compassion for others and help them to go forth not as bystanders, but as bold agents of the Holy Spirit. And as they stand up for others, Lord, I will have peace knowing that You are protecting them. In Jesus' mighty name I pray, Amen!

TIPS AND RESOURCES FOR YOUR CHILDREN – BULLYING AND THE BYSTANDER

Memory Verse: Do what is right and good in the Lord's sight so that it may go well with you (Deuteronomy 6:18 NIV).

What to do as a Bystander:

1. Pray to the Lord for help.

2. Never join in.

3. Don't just stand there and give the impression that you approve.

4. Defend the person being bullied if it won't put you in danger.

5. If the situation is too dangerous to intervene, then immediately tell a trusted adult (ask to remain anonymous if you feel threatened).

6. Reach out to the victim.

Help Lines:

1-800-273-TALK	The Lifeline
1-866-444-6996	Anti-Bullying Hotline
1-800-784-2433	National Hopeline
1-800-273-TALK	National Suicide Prevention Hotline

Links:

http://www.pacer.org/bullying/video/player.asp?video=69

www.bullyfreekids.com

www.eyesonbullying.org

Sword of the Spirit:

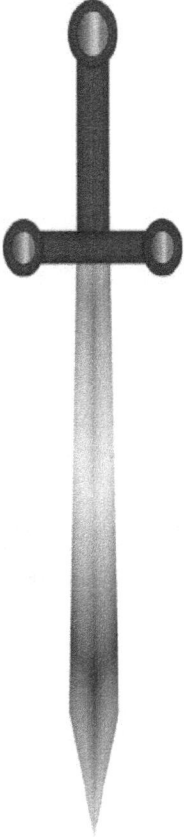

Love your neighbor the same as you love yourself (Luke 10:27).

The wicked flee when no one pursues, but the righteous are bold as a lion (Proverbs 28:1 ESV).

For you will be treated as you treat others. The standard you use in judging is the standard by which you will be judged (Matthew 7:2 NLT).

Don't be afraid of those who want to kill your body; they cannot touch your soul. Fear only God, who can destroy both soul and body in hell (Matthew 10:28 NLT).

The fear of man lays a snare, but whoever trusts in the Lord is safe (Proverbs 29:25 ESV).

Do all that you can to live in peace with everyone (Romans 12:18 NLT).

I called to the LORD for help, and he saved me from my enemies! He is worthy of my praise! (Psalm 18:3)

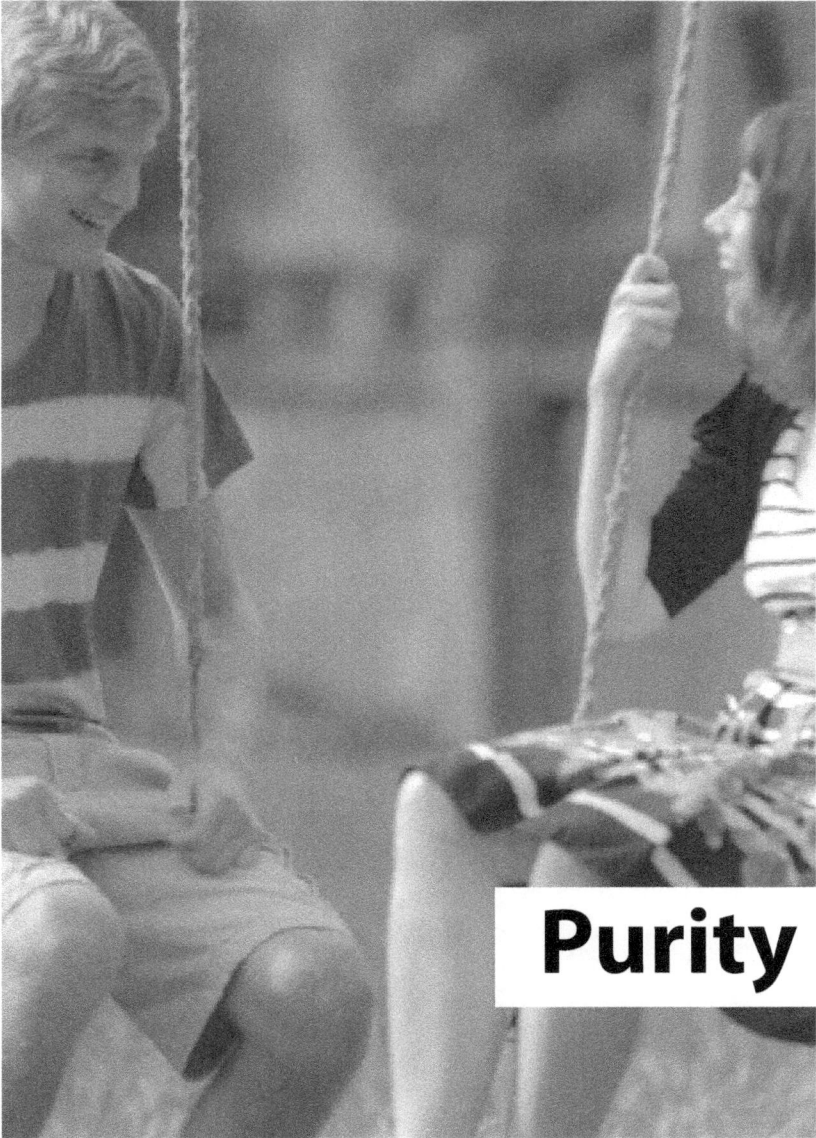

Purity

PURITY

Bible References Genesis 39:1–2, 6–12; Romans 12:2, 8:38–39, 10:9; 1 Thess. 4:3–8; 1 Cor. 6:13,18, 20, 10:13; Matthew 15:19–20; Proverbs 4:23, 5:21; 1 John 1:9; 1 Timothy 4:12; Deut. 6:18; 2 Cor. 5:17; Psalm 51:10

> **Memory Verse:** God paid a very high price to make you his. So honor God with your body (1 Corinthians 6:20).

✝ **Opening Prayer** – Lord, open my heart to receive the truth of Your Word, Amen!

Watch PURITY–LESSON Video Clip

SETTING THE PACE – Your Thoughts and Experiences/ Discussion Group

1. Why should teens remain pure when everyone else seems to be "doing it?"

2. What are some consequences for not remaining pure?

3. What could girls and guys do to help each other stay committed to purity?

4. What do you hope the opposite sex would notice about your child?

RUNNING THE RACE – Study

Sex sells. It's used to sell fast food, bottled water, jeans, deodorant, cars, and just about everything else. It's rampant in movies and television, and it appears that everyone is "doing it." While the world may think that's the acceptable thing to do, what does God say about it?

God created sex and sex is good, but He designed it to be beautiful between a man and a woman in marriage. It's to keep a husband and wife intimate with each other and to procreate—to have babies and populate the world. Sex in itself isn't bad. It's when people misuse it in ways that God didn't intend that it turns into sin. Let's look at two different examples in the Bible of how sex was handled.

In the Book of Genesis, Joseph had been sold as a slave by his brothers:

> The traders who bought Joseph took him down to Egypt. They sold him to the captain of Pharaoh's guard, Potiphar. The Lord helped Joseph become a successful man. Joseph lived in the house of his master, Potiphar the Egyptian....
>
> Joseph was a very handsome, good-looking man. After some time, the wife of Joseph's master began to pay special attention to him. One day she said to him, "Sleep with me."
>
> But Joseph refused. He said, "My master trusts me with everything in his house. He has given me responsibility for everything here. My master has made me almost equal to him in his house. I cannot sleep with his wife! That is wrong! It is a sin against God."
>
> The woman talked with Joseph every day, but he refused to sleep with her. One day Joseph went into the house to do his work. He was the only man in the house at the time. His master's wife grabbed his coat and said to him, "Come to bed with me." But Joseph ran out of the house so fast that he left his coat in her hand (Genesis 39:1-2, 6-12).

A young, single guy in his twenties, "Joseph was a very handsome, good-looking man." He was probably lonely, being in a foreign land away from his family and all that he knew. He had a very important woman wanting him. It could have been easy for him to fall into temptation. And this wasn't a one-time event. She seduced him "every day." But Joseph had made up his mind that he was going to remain pure and he stuck to it. In fact, he ran from the situation. Sometimes we just have to make up in our minds to do whatever it takes, to run so fast from anything that would get us to compromise. We have to look beyond the moment to the bigger picture. Joseph understood that his master trusted him and he shouldn't break that trust. He knew it would be a sin against God. Joseph didn't allow emotions to rule him. He took the time to rationalize the situation and God honored him for his right decisions. In fact, Joseph eventually became second in command only to the Pharaoh.

King David, on the other hand, didn't flee. He ran to his desire. He went with his emotions and when he saw a beautiful woman, he slept with her. Bathsheba became pregnant, and as it often happens, David had no plans to marry her. Instead he tried to trick Bathsheba's husband, who was a soldier and abstaining from sex during battle, to sleep with her so everyone would believe that Bathsheba had become pregnant by her husband, and David would be off the hook. But the husband remained honorable, so King David had him killed on the front lines. Giving into his desires had caused David to become a murderer besides an adulterer. After killing her husband, King David ended up marrying Bathsheba, but think about how she must have felt. She had not only lost her husband, but the king was marrying her because he had no other choice. Furthermore, God did not honor their decisions. They paid dearly for their sins, and their baby died.

Romans 12:2 says, "Don't change yourselves to be like the people of this world," and you should remind your children that they are not to buckle under peer pressure and act like everyone else. Just because it seems to be the popular thing to do, the cost of sin outside of marriage is high. Couples marry prematurely and end up divorced. Countless babies are aborted every year. There is the very real problem of sexually transmitted diseases. A person's reputation may suffer. And since we serve an all-holy God, His full blessings cannot be on a relationship that is based on sin. The Bible says:

> God wants you to be holy. He wants you to stay away from sexual sins. God wants each one of you to learn to control your own body. Use your body in a way that is holy and that gives honor to God. Don't let your sexual desires control you like the people who don't know God. Never wrong any of your fellow believers or cheat them in this way. The Lord will punish those who do that. We have already told you this and warned you about it. God chose us to be holy. He does not want us to live in sin. So anyone who refuses to obey this teaching is refusing to obey God, not us. And God is the one who gives you his Holy Spirit (1 Thessalonians 4:3-8).

The Bible also instructs: "The body is not for sexual sin. The body is for the Lord, and the Lord is for the body (1 Corinthians 6:13). "God paid a very high price to make you his. So honor God with your body" (1 Cor. 6:20). Our bodies are not our own to do as we please. They are the temple of God and they belong to Him. But how can your children honor God?

1 Corinthians 6:18 warns everyone to "run away from sexual sin. It involves the body in a way that no other sin does. So if you commit sexual sin, you are sinning against your own body." Share with your children that, yes, it is hard to run like Joseph did. Yet, 1 Corinthians 10:13 assures each of us that "the only temptations that you have are the same temptations that all people have. But you can trust God. He will not let you be tempted more than you can bear. But when you are tempted, God will also give you a way to escape that temptation. Then you will be able to endure it."

An anonymous writer described it this way: "If you have been tempted into evil, flee from it. It is not by falling into the water but by lying in it, that one drowns." Pastor and author Rick Warren said, "Ignoring a temptation is far more effective than fighting it. Once your mind is on something else, the temptation loses its power. So when temptation calls you on the phone, don't argue with it, just hang up."

Our children must hang up and take control of their thoughts. "All these bad things begin in the mind: evil thoughts, murder, adultery, sexual sin, stealing, lying, and insulting people" (Matthew 15:19-20). Share with them that the mind is satan's playground and we cannot allow him to rule. If we can control our mind, then we can overcome our emotions. Proverbs 4:23 reminds us: "Above all, be careful what you think because your thoughts control your life."

When your children say, "but we love each other," remind them that if they really love each other then they should want the full blessings of the Lord on their relationship and to wait until they are married. Anyone who tries to persuade otherwise by "if you really loved me you would do this," doesn't really love him/her. That person wants the instant gratification, not the lifetime commitment.

When your children share that part of themselves with someone, they can never get that back. Virginity can't be re-gifted. If that person turns out not to be their future husband or wife, they will never be able to share that special gift with their true mate. Not only that, but if your children choose to sleep with others before their perspective husband or wife, they also sleep with every person the other one has ever been with, along with everyone each of them have. It's a scary reality.

However, if they conduct themselves in the way God intended, and are only ever with the one person who is their husband or wife, then the risk of sexually transmitted diseases doesn't exist. It's when they step out of God's plan that there are chances of risks with serious consequences. But "when you decide to lead a clean life, chastity will not be a burden on you; it will be a crown of triumph" (Priest St. Josemaria Escriva).

Here are some practical tips to share with your children to help them remain pure:

- Date people who have the same values, and set ground rules at the beginning of your relationship.

- Girls should watch how they dress and act so they don't give others the wrong impression. Inspirational speaker, Lisa Bevere, put it this way: "If you want a guy to appreciate you for your mind, don't overwhelm him with your cleavage and navel. Your point will be lost."

- Respect each other. Work on getting to know that person better not in the physical sense, but by becoming best friends with him or her—knowing every intimate detail in the mental sense.

- Avoid being in tempting situations.

- Group date.

- Pace yourself. Don't allow moments to get too passionate. Keep the big picture in mind.

- Make a plan so you aren't caught off guard.

- Have an accountability partner.

- Take all impure thoughts captive and pray to Christ to keep you strong.

- Pray before each date.

- Keep in mind that the Lord is on every date with you. Proverbs 5:21 says, "The Lord clearly sees everything you do. He watches where you go." For a quick, cold shower, just think of Jesus being in the sack with both of you.

Mary managed to stay pure even though she had a serious boyfriend. She and Joseph were engaged to be married. Yet Mary remained a virgin and was able to become the mother of Jesus. The Lord really blessed her steadfastness!

What if you find out that your children have already gone too far? If that's the case, encourage them to not feel like they might as well continue because they already blew it. It's true that we can only lose our virginity once, and unfortunately that's something no one can change. They will have to live with the consequences of their actions, but God will forgive them when they confess their sins to Him and stop doing what they were doing. And to their future spouses, the less transgressions they have to confess, the better. Even though to another they won't be a virgin again, to God they will be clean and as white as snow. 1 John 1:9 says, "But if we confess our sins, God will forgive us. We can trust God to do this. He always does what is right. He will make us clean from all the wrong things we have done."

They still have worth and not even sexual sin can separate them from God's unfailing love. His Word promises us in Romans 8:38-39: "Yes, I am sure that nothing can separate us from God's love—not death, life, angels, or ruling spirits. I am sure that nothing now, nothing in the future, no powers, nothing above us or nothing below us—nothing in the whole created world—will ever be able to separate us from the love God has shown us in Christ Jesus our Lord." Praise God for second chances!

The key is for them to remember their purpose in life and who they are in Christ. They are princesses or princes of the King, so they should treat themselves with respect. 1 Timothy 4:12 says, "You are young, but don't let anyone treat you as if you are not important. Be an example to show the believers how they should live. Show them by what you say, by the way you live, by your love, by your faith, and by your pure life." Mother Teresa said, "To be pure, to remain pure, can only come at a price, the price of knowing God and loving him enough to do his will. He will always give us the strength we need to keep purity as something beautiful for God. Purity is the fruit of prayer."

Watch TESTIMONY–PURITY Video Clip

PREPARING FOR THE FINISH LINE – Invitation
It's tough to be role models for our children without the strength and

guidance of the Holy Spirit. If you haven't accepted Jesus into your life before, but would now like Him to be your accountability partner, please repeat this prayer:

Lord Jesus, I am too weak to overcome the sins of this world, and I ask You to take over and help me to be strong. Please forgive me for all of my sins. I believe in my heart and confess with my mouth that You are the Son of the Most High God.1 Wash my heart and make it clean and help me to live a life that is pleasing to You. Thank You, Jesus, for Your gift of eternal life. In Christ's name I pray, Amen!

🎵 WORSHIP – Listen to the Song *WAIT*

👟 ENDURANCE – Closing Prayer

Heavenly Father, I praise You for being the creator of intimacy and of marriage, and that if I teach my children to follow Your perfect plan for relationships they won't have to worry about the sins of this world: diseases, untimely pregnancies, broken relationships, and especially a broken relationship with You. Lord, please give my children the strength to wait and to overcome temptation. Help them to "do what is right and good in the Lord's sight"2 and to overcome the desires of the flesh. Keep them pure and clean as a bride of Christ. Help them to resist buying into the world's lifestyle, and place a hedge of protection around all of their thoughts and eyes. And if they have fallen short, Lord, please give them the power to stop and to turn back to You, and give me the wisdom to deal with the situation. Thank You that "[a]nyone who belongs to Christ is a new person. The past is forgotten, and everything is new."3 "Create in [us] a pure heart, O God, and renew a steadfast spirit within [us]."4 In Jesus' precious, holy name I pray, Amen!

TIPS AND RESOURCES – PURITY

Memory Verse: God paid a very high price to make you his. So honor God with your body (1 Corinthians 6:20).

Purity Guidelines:

1. Pray to the Lord for help.
2. Date people who have the same values, and set ground rules at the beginning of your relationship.
3. Watch how you dress and act so you don't give someone the wrong impression.
4. Respect each other. Work on getting to know that person better not in the physical sense, but by becoming best friends with him or her–knowing every intimate detail in the mental sense.
5. Avoid being in tempting situations.
6. Group date.
7. Pace yourself. Don't allow moments to get too passionate. Keep the big picture in mind.
8. Make a plan so you aren't caught off guard.
9. Have an accountability partner.
10. Take all impure thoughts captive and pray to Christ to keep you strong.
11. Pray before each date.
12. Keep in mind that the Lord is on every date with you. Proverbs 5:21 says, "The Lord clearly sees everything you do. He watches where you go." For a quick, cold shower, just think of Jesus being in the sack with both of you.

Help Lines:

1-866-331-9474	National Teen Dating Abuse Hotline
1-877-332-7333	Real Help for Teens Hotline
1-800-232-4636	Nat'l STD and AIDS Hotline

Links:

http://studentdevos.com/how-do-you-know-if-sexual-purity-is-right-for-you/

http://purefreedom.org/7-secrets-to-purity-for-every-teen-girl/

http://www.christianitytoday.com/iyf/hottopics/sexabstinence/10-ways-to-practice-purity.html

Sword of the Spirit:

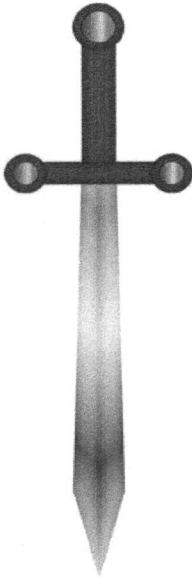

Great blessings belong to those whose thoughts are pure. They will be with God (Matthew 5:8).

Marriage should be honored by everyone. And every marriage should be kept pure between husband and wife. God will judge guilty those who commit sexual sins and adultery (Heb. 13:4).

So run away from sexual sins. It involves the body in a way that no other sin does. So if you commit sexual sin, you are sinning against your own body (1 Corinthians 6:18).

Create in me a pure heart, O God, and renew a steadfast spirit within me (Psalm 51:10 NIV).

Eating Disorders

EATING DISORDERS

Bible References 1 Samuel 16:7; 1 Peter 3:3–4; Isaiah 53:2, 40:29; Proverbs 31:30; Psalm 139:13–14; Romans 12:1; Ephesians 5:29–30; Song of Solomon 4:7; Matthew 6:25; 2 Corinthians 10:5; Jeremiah 31:3

Memory Verse: People judge others by what they look like, but I judge people by what is in their hearts (1 Samuel 16:7 CEV).

✝ **Opening Prayer:** Lord, guide me to delight in Your Word and Your promises, Amen!

Watch EATING DISORDERS–LESSON Video Clip

SETTING THE PACE – Your Thoughts and Experiences/ Discussion Group

1. Have you ever felt pressured to look a certain way? How did you deal with it?

2. Do you feel your children are being pressured?

3. The media hypes thinness. How do you think this feeds into eating disorders?

4. Name some famous actresses who are overweight.

5. Name some famous actresses who are thin.

6. Which list was easier to come up with?

7. Name some eating disorders.

8. What are some signs of an eating disorder?

9. Thinking about it now, have you noticed any of these signs with your children or their friends?

10. Why do you think some people develop eating disorders?

11. Have you ever known someone with an eating disorder?

12. If so, what happened with this person?

13. Have you ever skipped meals trying to lose weight?

14. Have you noticed any of your children being concerned about losing weight?

15. Is it true that people with eating disorders are always underweight?

16. How can sports play a part in eating disorders?

17. What are some problems that eating disorders can cause?

18. Can eating disorders cause death?

RUNNING THE RACE – Study

What do Mary-Kate Olsen, Lady Gaga, Oprah Winfrey, Dennis Quaid, Demi Lovato, Elton John, Paula Abdul, Snooki Polizzi, Kelly Clarkson, and Amanda Bynes all have in common? They each have suffered from an eating disorder. Singer Karen Carpenter, actresses Margaux Hemmingway and Karla Alvaraz, gymnast Christy Henrich, and ballet dancer Heidi Guenther are just a few who have died from the disease.

They're not alone. Approximately twenty-four million Americans battle eating disorders, and these disorders have the highest mortality rate of any mental health disease in American (National Eating Disorders Association). While 50 to 60 percent of teenage American girls believe they're overweight, only 15-20 percent of them actually are overweight.[1] What extremes do some go to in an effort to get what they think is the perfect body?

The two most common eating disorders are anorexia and bulimia. People suffering with anorexia don't see themselves as they really are. They believe they are fat even if they are severely underweight. They basically starve themselves by severely restricting their calorie intake, taking diet pills and laxatives, and exercising excessively. Food is their enemy, and sadly, 5-10 percent of anorexics die within 10 years, 18-20 percent within 20 year, and only 30-40 percent ever fully recover (National Association of Anorexia Nervosa and Associated Disorders).

Bulimia, on the other hand, involves binging and purging. People will overeat and then attempt to remove the food from their bodies through throwing up, laxatives, excessive exercise or other methods. Bulimics often have an average body weight but obsess about being thinner. Bulimia is harder to detect because the person will often look normal, but it's just as dangerous. Slow heart rate, damage to organs, stomach problems, tooth decay and dehydration are just a few of the problems associated with these eating disorders.[2]

So why are teens ruining their bodies in an effort to look good? Some have perfectionist problems, low self-esteem, or serious problems at home or in their personal lives that they don't know how to handle. If they can't control what's going on around them, they feel they can at least control what happens to their bodies.

Also, some believe lies that are spoken over them. When opening up about her struggles with an eating disorder, "Girls" actress Zosia Mamet said, "I was told I was fat for the first time when I was eight. I'm not fat; I've never been fat. But ever since then, there has been a monster in my brain that tells me I am. At times it has forced me to starve myself, to run extra miles, to abuse my body."[3]

Another reason is that our society places excessive value on looks, and the media hypes what they determine is beautiful. Zosia also commented on our culture's fixation with being skinny: "Society says, 'Hey, how about controlling the way you look? Skinny is beautiful.' Your obsession feels justified. It's no secret that we live in a country with a warped view of beauty."3 While the media promotes unrealistic standards, it's taking a destructive toll on people mentally and physically.

Actress Diane Keaton had to have all of her teeth recapped after bulimia destroyed them. Actress Thandie Newton said, "I've still got the scars on my knuckles from where I put my fingers down my throat." Singer and actress Paula Abul confided, "It is one of the toughest things to talk about, bar none, and it is one of the hardest disorders to deal with because it's not black or white. Eating disorders really have nothing to do with food, it's about feelings." And Diana Princess of Wales shared that same viewpoint in an interview about her struggles:

I had bulimia for a number of years. And that's like a secret disease. You inflict it upon yourself because your self-esteem is at a low ebb, and you don't think you're worthy or valuable. You fill your stomach up four or five times a day—some do it more—and it gives you a feeling of comfort. It's like having a pair of arms around you, but it's temporarily, temporary. Then you're disgusted at the bloatedness of your stomach, and then you bring it all up again. And it's a repetitive pattern, which is very destructive to yourself (1995 BBC Interview).

Maybe your children are struggling to see themselves as the beautiful people they really are, and maybe you have even had difficulties in this area. Your children may find it hard to imagine that they are God's cherished creation and even question why He didn't give them a thinner frame, smoother hair, bigger eyes, or a smaller nose. However, if your children are focusing on their shortcomings, have them consider Nick Vujicic.

Nick was born without limbs. He has no arms and no legs. There is no medical reason for his condition. That's just the way he is. Obviously he's had to overcome quite a bit in his life. Yet he remains positive and has become a true inspiration to others. He fishes, plays soccer and golf, and has a beautiful wife and son. He is president of Attitude is Altitude, has a DVD called No Arms, No Legs, No Worries, and has written several inspirational books. Although he struggled during his childhood years, at 15 he gave his life to Christ and started focusing on what he has instead of what he doesn't have. His advice is: "Dream big, my friend and never give up. We all make mistakes, but none of us are mistakes."4

No matter what we feel our flaws are when it comes to looks, since God created each of us in His image He is the judge of beauty and He says, "People judge others by what they look like, but I judge people by what is in their hearts" (1 Samuel 16:7 CEV). Again He says, "Don't be concerned about the outward beauty that depends on jewelry, or beautiful clothes, or hair arrangement. Be beautiful inside, in your hearts, with the lasting charm of a gentle and quiet spirit that is so precious to God" (1 Peter 3:3-4 TLB). Clearly God cares about our hearts and our inner beauty. If God really cared about outer appearances Jesus would have been good-looking, but He wasn't. It says in Isaiah 53:2 that "He wasn't some handsome king. Nothing about the way he looked made him attractive to us" (CEV).

That really doesn't stop any of us from wanting to look good, and we should always try our best at everything we do. It is not wrong to take care of ourselves but we are not to go to extremes and make our weight or other features our god. Happiness is not found in our outward appearance but in our relationship with Christ. "Charm can be deceiving, and beauty fades away, but a woman who honors the Lord deserves to be praised" (Proverbs 31:30 CEV). We are to turn to God for affirmation of our worth, and be willing to accept the things we can't change, knowing that we are God's workmanship.

While your children may not like what they see in the mirror right now, teach them to declare to the Lord as David did: "You are the one who put me together inside my mother's body, and I praise you because of the wonderful way you created me" (Psalm 139:13-14 CEV). As they praise our Creator, they will begin to see what God means when He assures us in Song of Solomon 4:7 that "[y]ou are altogether beautiful, my love; there is no flaw in you" (ESV).

It is essential to break the bondage of eating disorders not only for health purposes, but also because the Bible says we are "to offer [our] bodies as a living sacrifice, holy and pleasing to God" (Romans 12:1 NIV), and that "no one ever hated their own body, but they feed and take care of their body, just as Christ does the church—for we are members of his body" (Ephesians 5:29-30 NIV). To treat our bodies any differently goes against biblical principles.

If you are concerned that your children might be struggling in this area, here are some warning signs:

1. Excessive concern about weight and body shape
2. Unexpected weight loss
3. Disappearing to the bathroom after meals
4. Secretive eating or discovery that food is missing
5. Hiding food in the pretense of eating it
6. Loss of menstrual cycles
7. Evidence of laxative abuse
8. Food group avoidance
9. Skipping meals
10. Avoiding eating in front of others.[5]

Eating disorders are very serious and can be life-threatening, so it's important to seek help. Intervention is crucial, as people with the disorder can't or won't see beyond themselves. When "Girls" star Zosia's father put her into treatment she shared: "It was the first time I realized this wasn't all about me. I didn't care if I died, but my family did. That's the thing about these kinds of disorders: They're consuming; they make you egocentric; they're all you can see."[3]

Here are some tips to share with your children or others who are struggling with an eating disorder:

1. Pray to the Lord for strength and a clear mind. Tell someone you trust who will support and encourage you.

2. Write down what you eat each day to help you see the reality of your eating habits. A nutritionist can help you create a healthy eating plan.

3. Journal your feelings. See a Christian counselor or psychiatrist to discover what the triggers may be.

4. Visit a doctor to see if there are any other medical reasons for your problems, along with treating any symptoms caused by the disorder.

5. Focus on the positive things about yourself.

6. Surround yourself with uplifting people and keep active.

7. For severe cases, hospitalization may be required.

Singer Geri Halliwell (Ginger Spice from Spice Girls) struggled with bulimia and she gave this advice:

I realized I couldn't control this monster anymore. I needed to find help. I can honestly tell you from personal experience, that worrying about an eating disorder can get you down. There's nothing to be ashamed about. You'll be amazed at the difference it'll make to your whole life if you tell someone you trust. There are lots of people who want to help and you really can't fight this one on your own. It might be a hard decision to make, to tell people and seek help but, trust me it's nowhere as hard as trying to deal with it on your own.

Praise God that we never do have to deal with anything alone. God's Word says, "He gives strength to the weary and increases the power of the weak" (Isaiah 40:29 NIV). Jesus tells us, "Do not worry about your life. Do not worry about what you are going to eat and drink. Do not worry about what you are going to wear. Is not life more important than food? Is not the body more important than clothes?" (Matt. 6:25 NLV).

The Lord points out that life is more important than food and it's interesting to note that food was involved in the very first sin that caused our death. God told Adam and Eve not to eat fruit from the tree of knowledge of good and evil or they would surely die, but they ate it anyway. Eve wanted to be like God, and girls today are still struggling with food and self-image. Satan distracted her with lies and he continues to do the same to us—both girls and guys. We must impress on our children to stop believing these lies of the enemy, and "demolish arguments and every pretension that sets itself up against the knowledge of God, and take captive every thought to make it obedient to Christ" (2 Corinthians 10:5 NIV).

Start now by helping them to realize that perfection is not found in the mirror, but it is only found in Christ. Teach your children to see themselves as God sees them and choose to believe who God says they are!

Watch TESTIMONY–EATING DISORDERS Video Clip

PREPARING FOR THE FINISH LINE – Invitation

If you are tired of believing the lies of the enemy and want to find rest in the love of the Lord, please repeat this prayer:

Jesus, I'm tired of trying to be perfect because I never will be in the flesh. I thank You that I simply have to believe that You are the risen King and that You have forgiven my sins. Thank You for loving me as I am. In Jesus' holy name I pray, Amen!

WORSHIP – Listen to the Song *YOU LOOKS GOOD ON YOU*

ENDURANCE – Closing Prayer

Heavenly Father, please help my children to love who they are. Open their eyes to see themselves as You see them—as beautiful creations made in Your image. Make them beautiful from the inside out and keep them from trying to measure up to the media's standard of perfection so they can boldly proclaim that "the LORD will perfect that which concerns [us]; Your mercy, O Lord, endures forever; Do not forsake the works of Your hands."6 And if there are times when I don't feel like I measure up either, please help me to feel worthy, Lord. Thank You that You have loved [us] with an everlasting love and have drawn us with loving-kindness.[7] I love You and praise You. It is in Jesus' name I pray, Amen!

TIPS AND RESOURCES - EATING DISORDERS

Memory Verse: People judge others by what they look like, but I judge people by what is in their hearts (1 Samuel 16:7 CEV).

Tips for dealing with eating disorders:

1. Pray to the Lord for help.
2. Tell someone you trust who will support and encourage you.
3. Write down what you eat each day. A nutritionist can help you create a healthy eating plan.
4. Journal your feelings. See a Christian counselor or psychiatrist to discover any triggers.
5. Visit a doctor to see if there are any other medical reasons for your problems, along with getting treatment for any symptoms caused by the disorder.
6. Focus on the positive things about yourself.
7. Surround yourself with uplifting people–keep active.

Help Lines:

1-800-931-2237	National Eating Disorders Association
1-877-332-7333	Real Help for Teens Hotline
1-615-831-6987	Mercy Ministries
1-800-RUNAWAY	National Runaway Switchboard 24/7 Confidential

Links:

www.nationaleatingdisorders.com
http://www.nimh.nih.gov/health/publications/eating-disorders/index.shtml
http://christiananswers.net/q-eden/eatingdisorders.html
http://www.olivebranchoutreach.com/resources.htm
www.1800runaway.org   Allows youth to leave messages for parents and parents to leave messages for their children.

Sword of the Spirit:

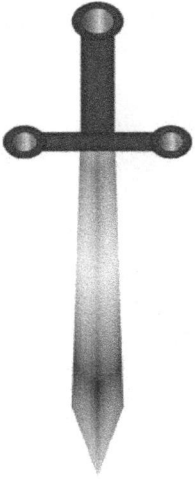

He gives strength to the weary and increases the power of the weak (Isaiah 40:29 NIV).

You are altogether beautiful, my love; there is no flaw in you (Song of Solomon 4:7 ESV).

You are the one who put me together inside my mother's body, and I praise you because of the wonderful way you created me (Psalm 139:13-14 CEV).

Charm can be deceiving, and beauty fades away, but a woman who honors the Lord deserves to be praised (Proverbs 31:30 CEV).

Substance Abuse

SUBSTANCE ABUSE

Bible References Proverbs 20:1, 23:19–21, 29–34, 23:32; Hosea 4:11; Esther 1:3–5, 7–8, 10–12, 2:1; Isaiah 28:1, 7; Ephesians 5:18; Galatians 5:16–17, 19–21; 2 Corinthians 5:17; James 1:12–17; Hebrews 12:1

Memory Verse: Don't be drunk with wine, because it will ruin your life. Instead let the Holy Spirit fill and control you (Ephesians 5:18 NLT).

✝ **Opening Prayer** – Lord, through Your Word deepen my understanding of Your truths and help me overcome, Amen!

Watch SUBSTANCE ABUSE–LESSON Video Clip

SETTING THE PACE – Your Thoughts and Experiences/ Discussion Group

1. What are some reasons teens drink and do drugs?

2. Name some different types of drugs.

3. Have you ever seen someone acting different when on drugs or alcohol? What things did they do?

4. What are some ways to avoid getting involved in drugs, smoking and/or alcohol?

5. What kind of wrong decisions could possibly be made while under the influence of drugs or alcohol?

6. What influences around you might contribute to drug use, alcohol consumption or smoking?

7. What are some effects of marijuana?

RUNNING THE RACE – Study

A teen and several of her friends were celebrating her 17th birthday at the home of a teenager whose father was out of town. Early the next morning a fire broke out while they were sleeping. The teen and five others were unable to escape due to the effects of drinking too much alcohol, and they perished.[1]

Convulsing, a teen lay on the ground, foaming at the mouth. Moaning and twitching, his tongue bleeding from being bitten during the convulsions, his friend held him in his lap, screaming for him to pull through as the friend waited for help from 911. The teen had seized for 45 minutes, and in the hospital his kidneys failed. Then his brain herniated, cutting off its blood supply. His pulse slowed and the tubes were removed. Bath salts had taken his life, much to the devastation of his best friend.[2]

Seeing a young woman struggling to change her SUV's tire on the side of the road, a youth pastor pulled over to help her, while a mother and her daughter came from a nearby home to also assist. Meanwhile, a sixteen-year-old driver with a blood alcohol content three times the legal limit was speeding down the road with seven teen passengers at 68-70 mph in a 40 mph zone. He crashed into the SUV, tragically killing all four and injuring everyone in the truck.[3]

A seventeen-year-old took 500 mg of Ecstasy and three LSD tablets. He then went online to chat with friends on Skype. His conversation became erratic, and he suddenly died of a drug overdose while his friends listened helplessly.[4]

Unfortunately, these tragic stories are true. Whether the substance abuse is alcohol, drugs or cigarettes, these activities can be deadly. Approximately 320,000 young people ages 15-29 die each year from alcohol-related causes.[5] The three leading causes of death for 15-24 year olds are auto crashes, homicides and suicides, and alcohol is the leading factor in all three.[6]

The number of teens dying from drug overdoses and abuse now exceeds the number of deaths from motor vehicle accidents in the U.S.,[7] while each day, more than 3,200 persons younger than 18 years of age smoke their first cigarette. Cigarette smoking causes 1,300 deaths every day. If smoking continues at the current rate among youth in this country, 5.6 million of today's Americans younger than 18 years of age will die prematurely from a smoking-related illness.[8]

That's a lot of death for causes that could be avoided. Whether a person's reason to drink, take drugs or smoke is to be cool, to have what he or she thinks is fun, or to deaden the pain, there can be serious consequences. Addiction is one of them. Health problems, poor academics, loss of friends, problems at home, and trouble with the law are just a few more. Some of us need to wise up.

Proverbs 20:1 says, "It isn't smart to get drunk! Drinking makes a fool of you and leads to fights" (CEV). Proverbs also warns:

> Listen, my child, be wise and give serious thought to the way you live. Don't associate with people who drink too much wine or stuff themselves with food. Drunkards and gluttons will be reduced to poverty. If all you do is eat and sleep, you will soon be wearing rags.
>
> Show me people who drink too much, who have to try out fancy drinks, and I will show you people who are miserable and sorry for themselves, always causing trouble and always complaining. Their eyes are bloodshot, and they have bruises that could have been avoided. Don't let wine tempt you, even though it is rich red, and it sparkles in the cup, and it goes down smoothly. The next morning you will feel as if you had been bitten by a poisonous snake. Weird sights will appear before your eyes, and you will not be able to think or speak clearly.

You will feel as if you were out on the ocean, seasick, swinging high up in the rigging of a tossing ship. "I must have been hit," you will say; "I must have been beaten up, but I don't remember it. Why can't I wake up? I need another drink." (23:19-21, 29-34 TEV)

"The Lord says, 'Wine, both old and new, is robbing my people of their senses!'" (Hosea 4:11 TEV). When we drink alcohol or take drugs, our minds don't think clearly and it's possible for wrong choices to be made, some even with deadly consequences as noted previously. In the Book of Esther, King Xerxes made a decision while he was drunk that he later regretted:

In the third year of Xerxes' rule, he gave a party for his officers and leaders. The army leaders and important leaders from all of Persia and Media were there. The party continued for 180 days. All during this time, King Xerxes was showing the great wealth of his kingdom and the majestic beauty and wealth of his palace. And when the 180 days were over, King Xerxes gave another party that continued for seven days. ...

Wine was served in golden cups, and every cup was different. There was plenty of the king's wine, because the king was very generous. The king had given a command to his servants. He told them that each guest must be given as much wine as he wanted, and the wine server obeyed the king. ...

On the seventh day of the party, King Xerxes was in high spirits from drinking wine. He gave a command to the seven eunuchs who served him.... He commanded them to bring Queen Vashti to him wearing her royal crown. She was to come so that she could show her beauty to the leaders and important people. She was very beautiful.

But when the eunuchs told Queen Vashti about the king's command, she refused to come. Then the king was very angry. (Esther 1:3-5; 7-8, 10-12)

The king gave a royal command that Vashti was never again to enter the presence of King Xerxes and that her royal position would be given to someone else. But "later, King Xerxes stopped being angry. Then he remembered Vashti and what she had done. He remembered his commands about her" (Esther 2:1).

After the king became sober, he missed his wife but couldn't take back the law he had decreed. Maybe if King Xerxes hadn't been drunk he wouldn't have made such a rash decision. Sadly, many of the wrong choices we make cannot be undone.

Isaiah Chapter 28 also records how Israel suffered from the errors of drunken leaders:

It is a time of trouble to the crown of pride and to the drunk men of Ephraim, whose shining beauty is a dying flower. It is at the head of the rich valley of those who have taken too much wine! ...

These also walk from one side to the other side because of wine and strong drink. The religious leaders and the men who tell what will happen in the future make mistakes because of strong drink. They are troubled by wine. They walk from side to side because of strong drink. They make mistakes as they have special dreams. And they make mistakes when judging between right and wrong. (28:1, 7 NLV)

Proverbs warns us that "[w]hile drinking might seem fun at the start, 'in the end it bites like a poisonous snake; it stings like a viper'" (23:32 NLT). Drugs affect our minds and bodies in a similar way, so these warnings apply to drug use also. We are not to be controlled by substances that might cause us to do ungodly things. Alcohol, drugs, and smoking are addictive and can tear up our bodies and minds, and rip apart our lives.

Many teens mistakenly believe that they are just having a good time experimenting with drugs and won't get addicted, but it actually can happen very easily because drugs change the way our brains work. Marijuana has the false reputation that it's not so bad, but teenagers are especially vulnerable to the effects of marijuana. About 60 percent of new users every year are under the age of 18, and two-thirds of adolescent substance treatment admissions are for marijuana.[9] Unless specifically prescribed to you by a doctor, all drug use is harmful, as well as alcohol consumption and cigarette smoking.

While smoking cigarettes may not alter your mind like drugs and alcohol, it is still very dangerous. Ninety percent of smokers began before the age of 21. According to the Surgeon General, teenagers who smoke are three times more likely to use alcohol, eight times more likely to smoke marijuana, and 22 times more likely to use cocaine. And if life isn't short enough already, on average, smokers die 13 to 14 years earlier than nonsmokers.[8] Is smoking a cigarette now really worth dying for later?

Are the drugs and alcohol worth ruining your life over? A teen shared on "PBS In the Mix" how his life got messed up by drugs:

> I started off smoking weed, and eventually it was just "alright", and familiar. I wanted something new. I've taken pretty much all of the club drugs there are....
>
> I got thrown into a pretty bad depression when I tried to go clean, and it didn't happen. I got thrown all out of whack, and I tried to kill myself. I remember I was just really, really feeling that this wasn't working, and had that little baby 'I don't wanna be here anymore' type of mentality. I wound up pouring gas all over myself and lighting it. I burnt 30% of my body.

The K-Hole. You're pretty much comatose. You don't want to do anything, you don't want to talk.

I think the biggest misconception about ecstasy would be "yeah, it's real". How do you know? It could be cut with anything, ranging from Ajax to rat poisoning. You have no idea what's in this thing you're about to take.

I was the type of person that you don't want to leave alone in your house. My parents would leave, and come back, and they'd be like "what did you take". I've actually had them pat me down.

All of us said the same thing: "I'm never gonna wind up in rehab." One of the hardest realizations I had was the fact that I had to ask for help no matter how much I didn't want to.[10]

CEO, S. Michael Houdmann, of GotQuestions.org said, "Any time spent kneeling before the god of drugs is time spent with your back towards the God of the Bible." It's time to turn around. If you or someone you know may be struggling with using drugs, alcohol or cigarettes, it's essential to get help. Substance abuse kills.

Being a teen can be tough, but none of these substances are the answer. Some ways to keep from getting involved with substance abuse is to avoid hanging out with the wrong crowd or being in a place where these activities will occur. Don't fall into temptation, because no matter how much you use drugs or drink alcohol, you'll still always feel empty. It is only the love of Christ and the Holy Spirit that fills you up. The Bible warns: "Don't be drunk with wine, because that will ruin your life. Instead, be filled with the Holy Spirit" (Ephesians 5:18 NLT). Galatians Chapter 5 states:

So I say, let the Holy Spirit guide your lives. Then you won't be doing what your sinful nature craves. The sinful nature wants to do evil, which is just the opposite of what the Spirit wants. And the Spirit gives us desires that are the opposite of what the sinful nature desires. These two forces are constantly fighting each other, so you are not free to carry out your good intentions. ...

When you follow the desires of your sinful nature, the results are very clear: sexual immorality, impurity, lustful pleasures, idolatry, sorcery, hostility, quarreling, jealousy, outbursts of anger, selfish ambition, dissension, division, envy, drunkenness, wild parties, and other sins like these. Let me tell you again, as I have before, that anyone living that sort of life will not inherit the Kingdom of God. (5:16-17, 19-21 NLT)

Don't follow that path of destruction, but walk instead with the Lord. If you've already strayed, however, it's okay because God can still set your feet on the right road. Instead of trying to hide from the pain and struggles of life through substance abuse, find your way with Jesus. Nothing is impossible with God, and through the Holy Spirit every chain of addiction can be broken. The Lord loves you so much that when you turn to Him, He will clean you up and give you a fresh new beginning. "Anyone who belongs to Christ is a new person. The past is forgotten, and everything is new" (2 Corinthians 5:17 CEV).

Pastor Harry Emerson Fosdick said, "No horse gets anywhere until he is harnessed. No steam or gas drives anything until it is confined. No Niagara is ever turned into light and power until it is tunneled. No life ever grows great until it is focused, dedicated, disciplined." It's time for us to discipline our lives.

Keep in mind that "[g]reat blessings belong to those who are tempted and remain faithful! After they have proved their faith, God will give them the reward of eternal life. God promises this to all people who love him. Whenever you feel tempted to do something bad, you should not say, 'God is tempting me.' Evil cannot tempt God, and God himself does not tempt anyone. You are tempted by the evil things you want. Your own desire grows until it results in sin" (James 1:12-17). So, let's fix our eyes on the prize of "great blessings" and "run with endurance the race that is set before us"[11] in healthy, whole bodies and only getting high on God's love.

Watch TESTIMONY–SUBSTANCE ABUSE Video Clip

PREPARING FOR THE FINISH LINE – Invitation

If you need the strength to break every chain of addiction or even the power to deal with everyday struggles, come to the only source strong enough to overcome everything in this world. Please repeat this prayer:

Jesus, I can't make it on my own. There are too many things in this world to overcome and I need You to rescue me from them all. I believe in my heart and confess with my mouth that You are the King of Kings and the Lord of my life.[12] I thank You that because You overcame death, that I too can overcome this world and be with You for eternity. Forgive me, Lord, for all of my sins. In Jesus' name I pray, Amen!

WORSHIP – Listen to the Song *MADE NEW*

ENDURANCE – Closing Prayer

Lord, this world is full of temptations—much more than I can ever handle on my own. Help me Jesus, to be more than a conqueror. Sometimes I am my own worst enemy and I ask You to tear down any strongholds within that may be hindering me. Protect me from the enemy who wants to destroy my body and my mind. Shield me from the temptations of this world. I offer my body to You as a dwelling place for the Holy Spirit. Thank You that You never give up on me, and that I can do all things through Christ Jesus who gives me the strength. Every chain is being broken, for in Jesus I am set free! Thank You, Lord. In Jesus' holy name I pray, Amen!

TIPS AND RESOURCES – SUBSTANCE ABUSE

Memory Verse: Don't be drunk with wine, because it will ruin your life. Instead let the Holy Spirit fill and control you (Eph. 5:18 NLT).

Tips to Avoid or Overcome Substance Abuse:

1. Pray to the Lord for help.
2. Avoid hanging out with the wrong crowd.
3. Don't be in a place where these activities will occur.
4. Before giving in to peer pressure, consider the costs and how it can destroy both you and your loved ones.
5. Get involved in positive activities that will keep you busy.
6. Substance abuse kills, so admit when you need help.
7. Join a support group.
8. Work with a professional counselor, pastor and/or rehabilitation center.
9. Engage with people who will support you and hold you accountable.
10. Remember, no matter how much you use drugs, smoke, or drink alcohol, you'll still always feel empty. It is only the love of Christ and the Holy Spirit that will fill you up.

Help Lines:

1-877-437-8422	Nat'l Drug and Alcohol Abuse Hotline
1-800-310-3001	Overcomers Outreach, Inc.
1-417-581-2181	Teen Challenge USA
1-615-831-6987	Mercy Ministries of America

Links:

www.mercymultiplied.com
www.overcomersoutreach.org
www.teenchallengeusa.com

Sword of the Spirit:

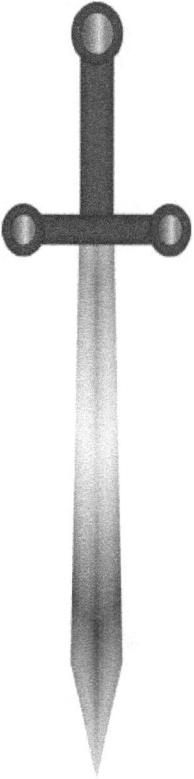

Anyone who belongs to Christ is a new person. The past is forgotten, and everything is new (2 Cor. 5:17 CEV).

I look up to the hills, but where will my help really come from? My help will come from the LORD, the Creator of heaven and earth (Psalm 121:1-2).

But the Lord is faithful. He will give you strength and protect you from the Evil One (2 Thessalonians 3:3).

So now anyone who is in Christ Jesus is not judged guilty (Romans 8:1).

No test or temptation that comes your way is beyond the course of what others have had to face. All you need to remember is that God will never let you down; he'll never let you be pushed past your limit; he'll always be there to help you come through it (1 Corinthians 10:13 MSG).

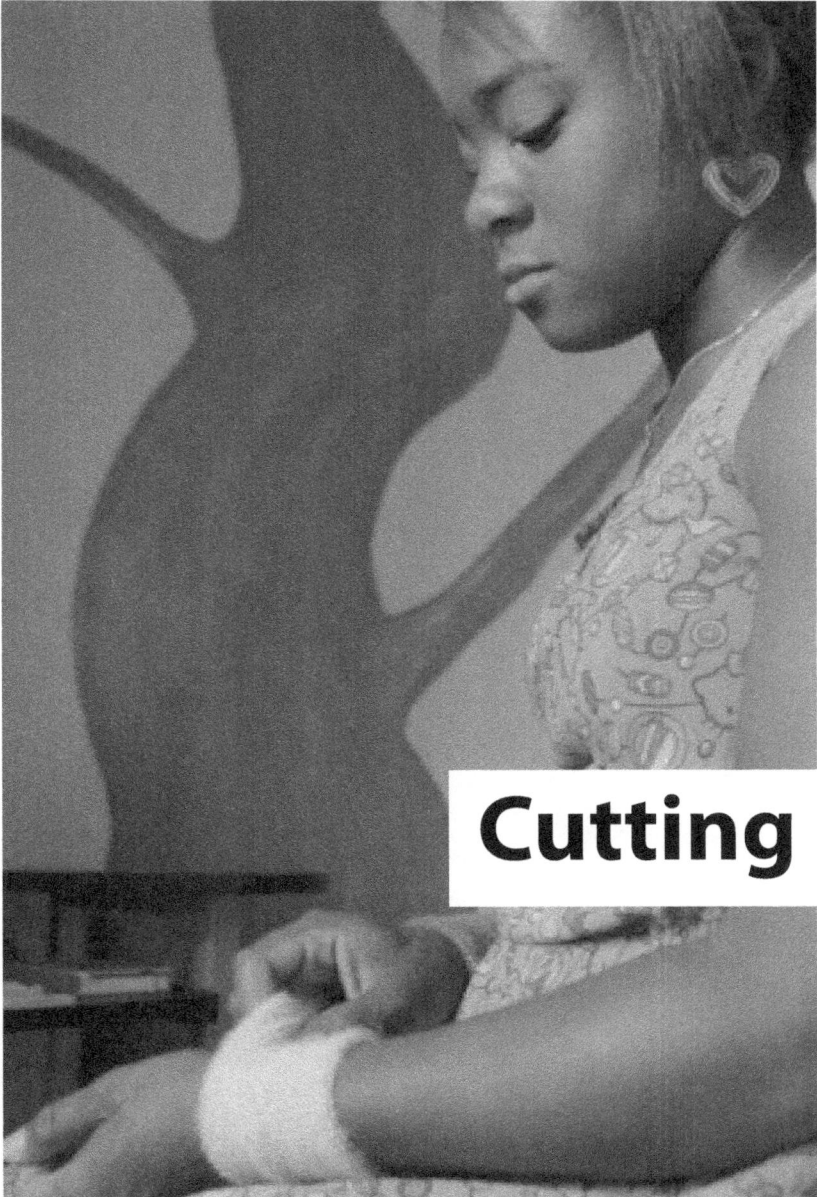

Cutting

CUTTING

Bible References Leviticus 21:5, 19:28; Deuteronomy 14:1; 1 Kings 18:26–28; Mark 5:2–5, 5:15; Isaiah 40:27–31, 41:10, 53:5; Matthew 11:28–29; Proverbs 14:13, 24:16; Psalm 147:3; Romans 8:38–39, 10:9

Memory Verse: He heals their broken hearts and bandages their wounds (Psalm 147:3).

✝ **Opening Prayer** – Lord, let Your Word fill my heart with joy, Amen!

Watch CUTTING–LESSON Video Clip

SETTING THE PACE – Your Thoughts and Experiences/ Discussion Group

1. What is self-injury and what types are there?

2. What areas of the body are most common for cutting?

3. Why do you think people self-injure?

4. What are some things that might trigger self-injury?

5. List activities that can help a person calm down.

6. True or false: Everyone who cuts is suicidal.

7. True or false: People who cut are seeking attention.

8. If you found out one of your friends was cutting, what would you say to him or her?

Cutting is a form of self-injury, or SI, and it's being dubbed "the new anorexia" because, like eating disorders, teens are using this form of self-harm to try to control painful emotions and intense pressure. While guys also struggle with self-mutilation, girls are especially prone to being cutters, and statistics show that approximately one in every 200 adolescent girls between 13 and 19 cut themselves on a regular basis.[1]

While cutting seems to be the latest fad, self-injury actually took place during bible times. Cutting was a pagan ritual and God makes it clear how He feels about it. In the Book of Leviticus, God gave Moses a list of practices that He commanded the Israelites not to do. Leviticus 21:5 states: "They must not make any cuts in their bodies." Deuteronomy 14:1 also orders: "You are the children of the LORD your God. Do not cut yourselves" (NIV).

There were several reasons back then why people cut themselves. The Bible tells that they did it as a mourning ritual. "You must not cut your body as a way to remember the dead" (Leviticus 19:28). Cutting was also used to worship the pagan god, Baal. In 1 Kings, Elijah and the prophets of Baal were having a showdown as to who was the true God by waiting to see which god would answer their prayers and start a fire for the sacrifice:

> So the prophets took the bull that was given to them and prepared it. They started praying to Baal and prayed until noon. They said, "Baal, please answer us!" But there was no sound. No one answered. Then they began jumping around on the altar they had built.
>
> At noon Elijah began to make fun of them. He said, "If Baal really is a god, maybe you should pray louder! Maybe he is busy. Maybe he is thinking about something, or maybe he stepped out for a moment! He

could be sleeping! Maybe you should pray louder and wake him up!" So the prophets prayed louder. They cut themselves with swords and spears. (This was the way they worshiped.) They cut themselves until they were bleeding all over. (18:26-28)

Why do people today cut themselves? Cutting is used by some as a way to cope with intense pressure from relationship problems, self-esteem issues, peer pressure, job stress, or bullying. They may suffer overwhelming sadness, anger, depression, loneliness, rejection, emptiness, self-hatred, or other emotions that they can't even name. Some people feel overcome and don't know how to handle these emotions. The pressure builds up inside so much that they resort to cutting as a way of letting it out.

While some will try cutting because friends pressure them to, usually it's not something that is premeditated. It often happens in a desperate moment when things are out of control and cutting seems like the only way to express the pain, relieve frustration, or even provide a distraction. Some feel they deserve the punishment. Others feel, like with eating disorders, that while they can't control the circumstances, they are at least in control of what they are doing to their bodies. And for those who feel totally numb to life, cutting is a way to make them feel again.

Contrary to belief, cutters are not usually suicidal. They are actually trying to feel better. However, the more it continues, the greater the chances are that they'll go too far and accidentally kill themselves. There's also the threat of infection, along with the psychological harm of the intense guilt and shame many feel. Most cutters suffer in silence. They aren't seeking attention—they are seeking relief.

Yet some celebrities such as Demi Lovato, Angelina Jolie, Russell Brand, and Fiona Apple have opened up about their struggles. In a 1995 BBC interview, Princess Diana said, "You have so much pain inside yourself that you try to hurt yourself on the outside because you want help." Author Amy Efaw, in her book titled *After*, shared her struggles with cutting this way: "In case you didn't know, dead people don't bleed. If you can bleed—see it, feel it—then you know you're alive. It's irrefutable, undeniable proof. Sometimes I just need a little reminder."

Unfortunately, that type of reminder can become an addiction. Cutting releases endorphins, the body's "feel good" chemicals, which act like a natural antidepressant. But then, whenever there's stress the brain craves this false sense of relief. It can become a hard habit to break and ends up controlling a person when the original intent was to gain control. So what can be done to stop this self-destructive cycle?

In New Testament times, the Bible records a time when Jesus came face-to-face with a cutter:

> When Jesus got out of the boat, a man came to him from the caves where the dead are buried. This man had an evil spirit living inside him. He lived in the burial caves. No one could keep him tied up, even with chains. Many times people had put chains on his hands and feet, but he broke the chains. No one was strong enough to control him. Day and night he stayed around the burial caves and on the hills. He would scream and cut himself with rocks. (Mark 5:2-5)

Jesus healed the man by casting out the evil spirits that were tormenting him. Then the townspeople "came to Jesus, and they saw the man who had the many evil spirits. He was sitting down and wearing clothes. He was in his right mind again" (Mark 5:15).

Today, we can receive the same healing through Jesus Christ. He says to us, "Don't worry—I am with you. Don't be afraid—I am your God. I will make you strong and help you. I will support you with my right hand that brings victory" (Isaiah 41:10). He also says, "If you are tired from carrying heavy burdens, come to me and I will give you rest" (Matthew 11:28-29 CEV). He knows your struggles and He knows your pain. He is there for you and He loves you with an everlasting love. You don't have to be perfect with Him. The Lord comes to you where you are, and He loves who you are for He created you.

Pray to Jesus when you get the urge to cut and He will give you the strength. And if you relapse, don't despair. The Lord assures us in Proverbs 24:16: "Good people might fall again and again, but they always get up. It is the wicked who are defeated by their troubles." Everyone who has accepted Christ and is in the family of God are the "good people" He is referring to, and even the good may have a setback but they go on. Don't allow guilt or shame to keep you from getting back up. In time you will learn to turn your worries over to Him and to love yourself as Jesus does.

While you grow stronger, if you need additional support when you have the urge to cut, try to distract yourself with something else. Here are some further ideas to help you:

- Pray and read your Bible
- Listen to soothing music
- Call a friend
- Play with a pet
- Relax with yoga or a bubble bath
- Exercise—go for a walk, run, or bike ride; dance
- Journal your feelings; scribble on paper; compose a song or poem
- Squeeze a stress ball or play doh[1]

If you really can't get relief from the above, here are substitutes for cutting:

- Wear a rubber band on your wrist and snap it when you get the urge to cut
- Draw on your skin with a red marker instead of cutting
- Rub an ice cube on your skin where you would normally cut (The Mental Health Foundation, UK)

Don't hesitate to seek professional help. Cutting can sometimes be associated with mental health issues. There's nothing wrong with getting medical treatment. God puts trained personnel in our lives to help us.

Maybe you aren't a cutter, but you just may be the person God wants to use to help someone else. As mentioned before, often self-injurers keep it a secret. Proverbs says that "[s]omeone who is laughing may be sad inside" (14:13 EXB). Here are some warning signs:

- Unexplained cuts, scars, or bruises, especially on wrists, arms, legs, thighs or chest
- Wearing long clothes, socks or wristbands that cover the body, even in warm weather
- Irritability/isolation
- Needing to be alone for long periods of time
- Withdrawn
- Unusual desire for privacy; not wanting to change in front of others

Pray for that person and urge her or him to find hope in Christ. Be the light in that person's darkness. Encourage the person to tell a trusted adult and seek medical attention if needed. It is important not to act shocked, but to appear calm and non-judgmental. Share with your friend that God is always right here beside us and He will get us through if we wait on Him. The Bible promises us:

> God doesn't come and go. God lasts. He's Creator of all you can see or imagine. He doesn't get tired out, doesn't pause to catch his breath. And he knows everything, inside and out. He energizes those who get tired, gives fresh strength to dropouts. For even young people tire and drop out, young folk in their prime stumble and fall. But those who wait upon God get fresh strength. They spread their wings and soar like eagles, they run and

don't get tired, they walk and don't lag behind (Isaiah 40:27-31 MSG).

Remember that God is bigger than our pain and He cares. "He heals their broken hearts and bandages their wounds" (Psalm 147:3).

Watch TESTIMONY–CUTTING Video Clip

PREPARING FOR THE FINISH LINE – Invitation

If you are overwhelmed with life and find it hard to love yourself, come to the One who loves you unconditionally, can lift you from the burden of despair, and can wipe away your tears and heal your scars. Please repeat this prayer:

Lord Jesus, I turn over all my hurts and sorrows to You. I believe that You died on the cross to take my pain and rose again to give me hope.[2] I ask You to come into my life and forgive me for all of my sins. Thank You, Jesus, for healing and for eternal life. In Your glorious name I pray, Amen!

WORSHIP – Listen to the Song *HIDING IN THE DARK*

ENDURANCE – Closing Prayer

Heavenly Father, I pray to have the power to understand the greatness of Your love—just how wide, how long, how high, and how deep that love is. I thank You that even when I feel unworthy and can't even love myself that You promise nothing can ever separate me from God's love—not death, life, angels, or ruling spirits—nothing in the future, no powers, nothing above us or nothing below us—nothing in the whole created world—will ever be able to separate me from the love God has shown me in Christ Jesus our Lord.[3] And because You are love, You wipe away every tear and mend every scar. Help me to deal with my pain and make me strong. I thank You that by Your wounds I am healed![4] In Jesus' name I pray, Amen!

TIPS AND RESOURCES – CUTTNIG

Memory Verse: He heals their broken hearts and bandages their wounds (Psalm 147:3).

How to distract yourself from self-injuring:
1. Pray and read your Bible
2. Listen to soothing music
3. Call a friend
4. Play with a pet
5. Relax with yoga or a bubble bath
6. Exercise—go for a walk, run, or bike ride; dance
7. Journal your feelings; scribble on paper; compose a song or poem
8. Squeeze a stress ball or playdoh

Substitutes for cutting:
1. Wear a rubber band on your wrist and snap it when you get the urge to cut
2. Draw on your skin with a red marker instead of cutting
3. Rub an ice cube on your skin where you would normally cut

*Seek professional help.

Help Lines:
1-800-DON'T-CUT	More Information on Self-Injury
1-800-273-TALK	24-Hour Crisis Hotline
1-800-334-HELP	Self-Injury Foundation's 24-Hour Nat'l Crisis Hotline

Links:
www.focusonthefamily.com/lifechallenges/abuse_and_addiction/
conqueringcutting.com
www.towriteloveonherarms.com
http://www.self-injury.org/

Sword of the Spirit:

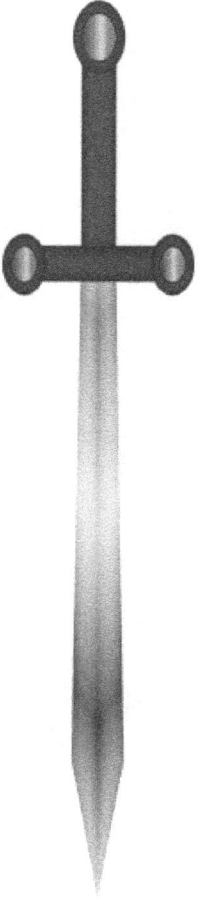

Don't worry—I am with you. Don't be afraid—I am your God. I will make you strong and help you. I will support you with my right hand that brings victory (Isaiah 41:10).

If you are tired from carrying heavy burdens, come to me and I will give you rest (Matthew 11:28-29 CEV).

God doesn't come and go. God lasts. He's Creator of all you can see or imagine. He doesn't get tired out, doesn't pause to catch his breath. And he knows everything, inside and out. He energizes those who get tired, gives fresh strength to dropouts. For even young people tire and drop out, young folk in their prime stumble and fall. But those who wait upon God get fresh strength. They spread their wings and soar like eagles, they run and don't get tired, they walk and don't lag behind (Isaiah 40:27-31MSG).

Good people might fall again and again, but they always get up. It is the wicked who are defeated by their troubles (Proverbs 24:16).

Abuse

ABUSE

Bible References 2 Samuel 13:1–2, 10–18; Ephesians 4:29; James 3:5–6; John 13:34, 1:11; Matthew 27:27–31, 39–40; Luke 23:39, 12:7; Mark 9:42; Psalm 34:18, 10:17–18, 139:3; Deuteronomy 31:6

Memory Verse: The Lord is close to the brokenhearted and saves those who are crushed in spirit (Psalm 34:18 NIV).

✝ **Opening Prayer** – Lord, let the Holy Spirit touch me in a powerful way during this study, Amen!

Watch ABUSE–LESSON Video Clip

SETTING THE PACE – Your Thoughts and Experiences/ Discussion Group

1. Why do you think some people are abusive?

2. Do you think anyone who abuses others is ever justified?

3. Do you think that those who have been abused will become abusers? If so, why?

4. Why do you think that so many victims of abuse keep quiet about it?

5. What are some ways a victim might escape an abusive situation?

6. What would you say to someone you know who is being abused, either physically, sexually or emotionally? How might you help them?

7. In what ways was Jesus abused?

🏃 RUNNING THE RACE – Study

In the movie, *Steadfast*, Claire, is the victim of emotional and physical abuse by her alcoholic father, and neglect from her mother who is also a drinker and struggles to deal with life. Like many victims of abuse, Claire, in turn, is abusive to others, especially Moriah. Anger, hurt, fear, and trust issues are just some of the problems that the abused face. Claire struggles with a myriad of insecurities, and it isn't until she accepts Christ as her Savior that she is finally free and can stand up to her father.

If you suffer from physical, emotional or sexual abuse, please know that you are not alone. According to statistics, there are over 6 million youth involved in reported child abuse cases every year.[1] Child abuse in the United States is so prevalent that:

- A report of child abuse is made every ten seconds.

- More than five children die every day as a result of child abuse.

Data on how this affects the victims is equally somber:

- About 30% of abused and neglected children will later abuse their own children.

- About 80% of 21 year olds that were abused as children had at least one psychological disorder.

- 14% of all men in prison in the USA were abused as children.

- 36% of all women in prison were abused as children.[2]

Sadly, many victims are being abused by their own parents, other family members or close friends. In fact, by eighteen years of age one in three girls and one in six boys will have been sexually abused by someone they know, love and trust.[3] In the Book of Second Samuel, King David's daughter was raped by her half-brother:

> David had a son named Absalom. Absalom had a very
> beautiful sister named Tamar. Another one of David's

sons, Amnon, was in love with Tamar. She was a virgin. Amnon wanted her very much, but he did not think it was possible for him to have her. He thought about her so much that he made himself sick. (13:1-2)

Amnon then plotted a way to get Tamar alone with him. He pretended to be sick and convinced King David to have Tamar cook food for Amnon and bring it to his sickbed. Tamar did as she was told and brought the food to the house of Amnon. He sent the servants away and called for Tamar:

Then Amnon said to Tamar, "Bring the food into the bedroom and feed me by hand."

So Tamar took the cakes she had made and went into her brother's bedroom. She started to feed Amnon, but he grabbed her hand. He said to her, "Sister, come and sleep with me."

Tamar said to Amnon, "No, brother! Don't force me to do this. Don't do this shameful thing! Terrible things like this should never be done in Israel! I would never get rid of my shame, and people would think that you are just a common criminal. Please, talk with the king. He will let you marry me."

But Amnon refused to listen to Tamar. He was stronger than she was, so he forced her to have sexual relations with him. Then Amnon began to hate Tamar. He hated her much more than he had loved her before. Amnon said to her, "Get up and get out of here!"

Tamar said to Amnon, "No! Don't send me away like this. That would be even worse than what you did before!"

But Amnon refused to listen to Tamar. He called his

servant and said, "Get this girl out of this room, now! And lock the door after her."

So Amnon's servant led Tamar out of the room and locked the door.

Tamar was wearing a long robe with many colors. The king's virgin daughters wore robes like this. Tamar tore her robe of many colors and put ashes on her head. Then she put her hand on her head and began crying.

Then Tamar's brother Absalom said to her, "Have you been with your brother Amnon? Did he hurt you? Now, calm down sister. Amnon is your brother, so we will take care of this. Don't let it upset you too much." So Tamar did not say anything. She quietly went to live at Absalom's house. (13:10-18)

Victims of sexual and physical abuse are threatened or told to keep quiet, and out of fear, shame, humiliation and guilt, they often comply. They suffer in silence, as do the victims of emotional abuse. Emotional abuse is particularly difficult to confront because the wounds are all on the inside. There is no bruising or other telltale marks—only inner scars. Yet this abuse is extremely dangerous because it eats away at a person's self-worth. God's Word warns people: "Don't use foul or abusive language. Let everything you say be good and helpful, so that your words will be an encouragement to those who hear them" (Ephesians 4:29 NLT).

Words are very dangerous and can cause a lot of damage. "A big forest fire can be started with only a little flame. The tongue is like a fire. It is a world of evil among the parts of our body. It spreads its evil through our whole body and starts a fire that influences all of life" (James 3:5-6). All of this is the opposite of the biblical principal Jesus laid out for us, which is to "[l]ove each other. You must love each other just as I have loved you" (John 13:34).

Yet Jesus himself suffered tremendous physical and verbal abuse. All throughout his ministry, people scorned him and plotted to kill him. John 1:11 says, "He came to the world that was his own. And his own people did not accept him." One of his own beloved disciples even turned Jesus in to be crucified. The abuse quickly escalated as he was about to be hung on the cross. The Bible reports:

> Then Pilate's soldiers took Jesus into the governor's palace. All the soldiers gathered around him. They took off Jesus' clothes and put a red robe on him. Then they made a crown from thorny branches and put it on his head, and they put a stick in his right hand. Then they bowed before him, making fun of him. They said, "We salute you, king of the Jews!" They spit on him. Then they took his stick and kept hitting him on the head with it. After they finished making fun of him, the soldiers took off the robe and put his own clothes on him again. Then they led him away to be killed on a cross. (Matthew 27:27-31)

As Jesus hung on the cross, "[p]eople walked by and shouted insults at Jesus. They shook their heads and said, 'You said you could destroy the Temple and build it again in three days. So save yourself! Come down from that cross if you really are the Son of God!'" (Matthew 27:39-40). "One of the criminals hanging there began to shout insults at Jesus: 'Aren't you the Messiah? Then save yourself, and save us too!'" (Luke 23:39).

Jesus suffered abuse and died on the cross to fulfill prophecy—to save us from our sins and to give us eternal life. However, as Moriah tells Claire in the movie, *Steadfast*, "Jesus' scars served a purpose, yours don't!" While Jesus does tell us to pick up our cross and follow Him, and warns that we will be persecuted and suffer trials, He doesn't mean for us to be abused in these manners. In fact, He warns against it in Mark 9:42: "[I]f you give one of these simple, childlike believers a hard time, bullying or taking advantage of their simple trust, you'll soon wish you hadn't. You'd be better off dropped in the middle of the lake with a millstone around your neck" (MSG).

Here are a few ways to deal with abuse:

1. If you are being harmed, seek help. Confide in someone you trust, such as a pastor, teacher, parent, or the authorities.

2. Family counseling may help emotional abuse situations.

3. Be aware of circumstances that may lead to sexual assault. If someone you trust becomes overly attentive you may need to stay away from that person, and tell someone immediately if you feel the situation could become dangerous.

4. If you know someone being abused, be there to support your friend. Listen and help your friend understand that it's not his or her fault. Encourage your friend to seek professional help. Report any physical or sexual abuse.

5. Don't argue with a drunk or drugged parent.

6. Don't tolerate abuse. Have a backup plan in case things get bad: plan a safe place to go to; keep emergency numbers on your phone; do what you need to be safe. You are not being disloyal by protecting yourself.

7. Ask God to give you the grace to forgive the abuser. This doesn't mean to excuse what he or she is doing and it doesn't mean that person is right. By forgiving, you are releasing that stronghold on your life. You are setting yourself free.

BE PRO-ACTIVE:

8. Don't share personal information with people you meet over the internet.

9. Never accept any type of open drink from someone. That is how some have been drugged and raped.

REMEMBER:

10. Abuse is never your fault. No one deserves to be abused, no matter what.

11. Never believe the negative words that are spoken over you. *You are not defined by what someone says or does to you.*

12. You are made in God's image, and God doesn't make junk.

13. Just because your own father may not treat you right, your heavenly Father cares for you with an unfailing love. He is faithful and can be trusted.

God's Word reassures us that "[t]he Lord is close to the brokenhearted and saves those who are crushed in spirit.... You listen to the longings of those who suffer. You offer them hope and you pay attention to their cries for help. You defend orphans and everyone else in need, so that no one on earth can terrify others again" (Psalm 34:18 NIV and 10:17-18 CEV).

You may have a hard time believing this if you've been a victim of abuse. You may even wonder if God is even paying any attention, but be assured that God has not abandoned you. He knows everywhere you go and everything you do (see Psalm 139:3). He even knows how many hairs you have on your head (see Luke 12:7) and He knows your pain. Abuse was not God's plan for you, but He created free will and evil exists in our world because of the choices others make. You won't always understand everything this side of heaven, but you must trust that God has a plan to restore your life.

An unknown author wrote a poem called *The Chosen Vessel* which describes just how the Lord cares for you:

> The Maker was searching for a vessel to use.
> Before Him were many, which one would He choose?
> "Take me," cried the gold one. "I'm shiny and bright,
> I'm of great value and I do things just right.

My beauty and luster will outshine the rest.

For someone like you, Master, gold would be best."

The master passed on with no word at all.

Then the Lord saw a graceful silver urn, along with a brass vessel polished like glass, a goblet of clear crystal, and a polished vessel of wood. He passed by all of them:

Then the Master looked down and saw a vessel of clay.

Empty and now broken, it helplessly lay.

No hope had the vessel that the Master might choose,

To cleanse and to make whole, to fill and to use.

"Ah! Now this is the vessel I've been hoping to find.

I'll mend it and use it and make it mine."

Then gently He "lifted up" the vessel of clay,

Mended and cleansed it and filled it that day:

He let the vessel know—"There's much work to do.

You are to pour out to others, as I pour into you."

Allow the Lord to take your brokenness and mold it into something beautiful. You, just as you are, is exactly what He is looking for. You are His chosen vessel. Let Him shape your life.

Watch TESTIMONY–ABUSE Video Clip

PREPARING FOR THE FINISH LINE – Invitation

If you are broken, take your scattered pieces now to the only One who can put everything back together and create something beautiful out of the rubble. Let Him love you as no one else in this world ever can. Even if you have never faced abuse but want the protection of the Lord over your life and have never accepted Christ, please repeat this prayer:

Lord, I turn my life over to You, to shape it into something beautiful as only You can. I believe in my heart and confess with my mouth that You took the abuse for me so that I may be free from sin and have eternal life.[4] *Please forgive me for any and all sins. Thank You, Jesus, for Your unfailing love. It is in Your holy name that I pray, Amen!*

🎵 WORSHIP – Listen to the Song *BROKEN CLAY*

👟 ENDURANCE – Closing Prayer

Heavenly Father, thank You for Your Word that encourages me to be strong and be brave, to not be afraid of those people because the LORD our God is with me. He will not fail me or leave me.[5] In You I have a spiritual Father who will always take care of me. In those times of darkness when maybe I don't always feel You there and I struggle to understand my circumstances, help me to feel Your loving arms around me and give me a peace that surpasses all understanding. Be my mighty fortress and my protector. I thank You, Daddy, for Your everlasting love. In Jesus' name I pray, Amen!

TIPS AND RESOURCES – ABUSE

Memory Verse: The Lord is close to the brokenhearted and saves those who are crushed in spirit (Psalm 34:18 NIV).

Tips for dealing with abuse:

1. If you are being harmed, seek help. Confide in someone you trust, such as a pastor, teacher, parent, or the authorities.
2. Family counseling may help emotional abuse situations.
3. Be aware of circumstances that may lead to sexual assault.
4. Don't isolate yourself from others—you need a support group.
5. If you know someone being abused, be there to support your friend. Listen and help your friend understand that it is not his/her fault. Encourage professional help.
6. Avoid arguing with a drunk or drugged parent.
7. Have a backup plan in case things get bad: plan a safe place to go to; keep emergency numbers on your phone; do what you need to be safe. You are not being disloyal by protecting yourself.
8. Ask God to give you the grace to forgive the abuser. This does not mean to excuse what he or she is doing and it doesn't mean that person is right. By forgiving, you are releasing that stronghold on your life. You are setting yourself free.

REMEMBER:

9. Abuse is never your fault. No one deserves to be abused.
10. Never believe the negative words that are spoken over you. *You are not defined by what someone says or does to you.*
11. You are made in God's image, and God doesn't make junk.
12. Just because your own father may not treat you right, your heavenly Father cares for you with an unfailing love. He is faithful and can be trusted.

Help Lines:

1-800-799-SAFE	National Domestic Violence Hotline
1-866-331-9474	National Teen Dating Abuse Hotline
1-877-332-7333	Real Help for Teens Hotline
800-4-A-CHILD	Childhelp Nat'l Child Abuse Hotline
1-888-290-7233	Safe Place

Links:

www.christianfaith.com/resources/abuse

www.christiananswers.net

www.childhelp.org

Sword of the Spirit:

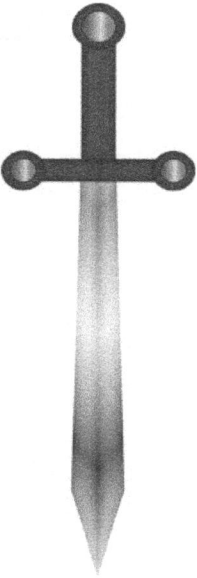

Yes, God even knows how many hairs you have on your head. Don't be afraid. You are worth much more than many birds (Luke 12:7).

For the wicked shall be destroyed, but those who trust the Lord shall be given every blessing (Psalm 37:9 TLB).

You protected me from violent enemies and made me much greater than all of them (Psalm 18:48 CEV).

When you talk don't say anything bad. But say the good things that people need—whatever will help them grow stronger. Then what you say will be a blessing to those who hear you (Ephesians 4:29).

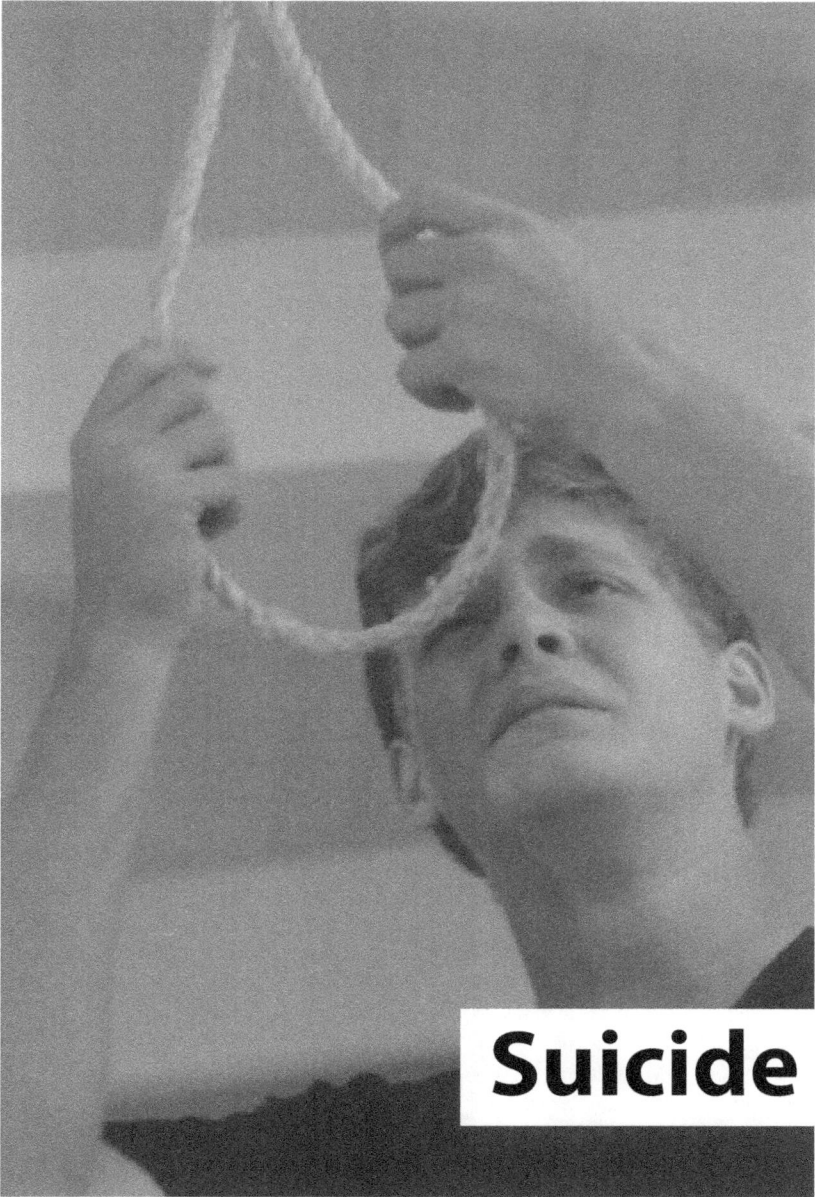

Suicide

SUICIDE

Bible References John 10:10, 8:44; Jeremiah 29:11; Judges 9:52–54, 16:28–30; 1 Samuel 31:4–5; 2 Samuel 17:23; 1 Kings 16:18, 19:4; Numbers 11:15; Job 6:8–9; Jonah 4:8; 2 Cor. 5:2; Psalm 33:20–22, 42:11, 40:1–3; Deut. 30:19–20; Col. 1:27; Matthew 27:3–5

Memory Verse: For I know the plans that I have for you, declares the Lord, plans to prosper you and not to harm you, plans to give you a hope and a future (Jer. 29:11 NIV).

Opening Prayer – Lord, stir hope within my heart through Your Word, Amen!

Watch SUICIDE–LESSON Video Clip

SETTING THE PACE – Your Thoughts and Experiences/ Discussion Group

1. Why do you think people decide life isn't worth living anymore?

2. Are there times when you feel like giving up? If so, what do you do to get through it?

3. If you think someone you know is considering suicide, should you tell someone?

4. What can you do to help a friend who is talking about suicide?

5. Have you known someone who committed suicide?

6. If so, how did it affect their family and friends?

7. What are your dreams and ambitions for your life?

8. What can you do to stay focused on your future goals?

There is a saying that suicide is a permanent solution to a temporary problem. It's true that problems are temporary, but suicide is not permanent. Our souls live forever either with the Lord in heaven, or in hell if we don't accept the gift of God's salvation, so death doesn't end things. Suicide does, however, end the chance for the unsaved to find salvation.

Suicide is the third leading cause of death among 15 to 24 year olds. Each year in the U.S., 2 million youth attempt suicide, while 2,000 ages 10-19 actually succeed.[1] Yet Jesus wants us to have life. In John 10:10 He says, "A thief comes to steal, kill, and destroy. But I came to give life—life that is full and good." The thief is satan and John 8:44 explains that satan is a murderer and the "father of lies." The hopelessness that leads to suicide is often a result of listening to those lies.

Just what are some of those lies? "Things will never get better." "Everyone would be better off without you." "No one will miss you anyway." "There's no hope—you'll never be happy again." "There's no way out." "You're better off dead." "Your problems are too big." "You have no other choice."

Angie Fenimore believed the lies when she committed suicide. In her book *Beyond the Darkness*, she tells of her experience in hell before she was miraculously brought back to life. Here are select excerpts:

> I was immersed in darkness. ...The darkness continued in all directions and seemed to have no end, but it wasn't just blackness, it was an endless void, an absence of light. It was completely enveloping.

> I swung my head around to explore the thick blackness and saw, to my right, standing shoulder to shoulder, a handful of others. They were all teenagers. ...the suicides. ...[They all] stood fixed in a thoughtless stupor. ...

Then God spoke to me.... "Is this what you really want? Don't you know that this is the worst thing you could have done?"

I could feel his anger and frustration, both because I had thrown in the towel and because I had cut myself off from him and from his guidance.

And I'd felt trapped. I had been able to see no other choice but to die before I could do any more damage in life. So I answered:

"But my life is so hard." ...

"You think that was hard? It is nothing compared to what awaits you if you take your life.... Life's supposed to be hard. You can't skip over parts. We have all done it. You must earn what you receive." ...

[Suddenly] I was painfully aware of the suffering I had caused my family and other people because of my own weaknesses. But now I saw that by ending my life, I was destroying the web of connections of people on earth, possibly drastically altering the lives of millions, for all of us are inseparably linked, and the negative impact of one decision has the capacity to be felt throughout the world.[2]

The *truth* is that suicide is a selfish act. While people committing suicide feel such hopelessness that they don't know how to live, death only brings more pain and problems by hurting other people. Things are never completely hopeless. We are never beyond the mercy and grace of the Lord. God created us in His image and He has a plan for our lives. "'For I know the plans I have for you,' declares the Lord, 'plans to prosper you and not to harm you, plans to give you hope and a future'" (Jeremiah 29:11 NIV).

But what about those who truly believe that they have no hope? This despair can come from many things: stress, low self-worth, bullying, pressure to succeed, fears of the future, failed relationships, physical or mental abuse, and many other problems that may overwhelm us to the point that we can't cope. And just as there has always been troubles in the world, the escape of suicide is also not new. There were seven people mentioned in the Bible who killed themselves.

Abimelech suffered from great pride. In Judges 9:52-54, after a woman dropped a grinding stone on Abimelech's head, he said to his servant, "Take out your sword and kill me. I want you to kill me so that people will not say, 'A woman killed Abimelech.' So the servant stabbed Abimelech with his sword, and he died."

King Saul felt rejected, alone, and a failure. During battle, "Saul told the boy who carried his armor, 'Take your sword and kill me or else these foreigners will do it and torment me as well!' But Saul's helper was afraid and refused to kill him. So Saul took out his own sword and fell on it. When the helper saw that Saul was dead, he took out his own sword, fell on it, and died there with Saul" (1 Samuel 31:4-5).

In 2 Samuel 17:23, Ahithophel became bitter when the people didn't do what he wanted them to. "When Ahithophel saw that the Israelites did not do what he suggested, he saddled his donkey and went back to his hometown. He made plans for his family and then hanged himself. They buried him in his father's tomb."

1 Kings 16:18 tells of the rebellious acts of a man named Zimri. During these events, "[w]hen Zimri saw that the town was captured, he ran into the strongest part of the palace and killed himself by setting it on fire" (CEV).

Samson died for revenge. While a captive of the Philistines in the temple, as they were laughing and making fun of him:

> Samson said a prayer to the LORD, "Lord GOD, remember me. God, please give me strength one more time. Let me do this one thing to punish these Philistines for tearing out both of my eyes!" Then Samson took hold of the two columns in the center of the temple that

supported the whole temple. He braced himself between the two columns. One column was at his right side and the other at his left side. Samson said, "Let me die with these Philistines!" Then he pushed as hard as he could, and the temple fell on the rulers and everyone in it. (Judges 16:28-30)

Perhaps the most famous suicide in the Bible was of Judas, the betrayer of Jesus. He suffered immense guilt:

Judas saw that they had decided to kill Jesus. He was the one who had handed him over. When he saw what happened, he was very sorry for what he had done. So he took the 30 silver coins back to the priests and the older leaders. Judas said, "I sinned. I handed over to you an innocent man to be killed." The Jewish leaders answered, "We don't care! That's a problem for you, not us." So Judas threw the money into the Temple. Then he went out from there and hanged himself. (Matthew 27:3-5)

While these men killed themselves, there were several other people in the Bible who wanted to die but didn't follow through with it. Moses said, "If this is the way you're going to treat me, just kill me now and end my miserable life!" (Number 11:15 CEV). Elijah "begged the LORD, 'I've had enough. Just let me die! I'm no better off than my ancestors'" (1 Kings 19:4 CEV). Job prayed, "How I wish that God would answer my prayer and do away with me" (Job 6:8-9 CEV). "[Jonah] shouted, 'I wish I were dead!'" (Jonah 4:8 CEV), and even the Apostle Paul said, "While we are here on earth, we sigh because we want to live in that heavenly home" (2 Corinthians 5:2 CEV). Yet all of them persevered. Unlike the others, they faced their difficulties and didn't give up.

How can we remain steadfast also? By remembering that we do have hope. Our hope comes from faith in God. "We wait in hope for the LORD; he is our help and our shield. In him our hearts rejoice, for we trust in his holy name. May your unfailing love be with us, LORD, even as we put our hope in you" (Psalm 33:20-22 NIV).

While God may not take us out of our troubles, He will always be with us through them. He is our ever-present help in times of trouble, and we, like King David, can say, "Why am I so sad? Why am I so upset? I tell myself, 'Wait for God's help! You will again be able to praise him, your God, the one who will save you'" (Psalm 42:11).

It is a cold, hard fact that suicide is a consequence that cannot be changed. Therefore, the threat of it must be taken seriously. If you or someone you know is contemplating suicide, immediate intervention is crucial. Suicide is rarely an impulsive decision. Depression has usually been building up over a long period of time, and this hopelessness often comes from not knowing any other way out. Most suicidal people don't actually want to die—they want their problems to end. Talk to someone who can help you to find other options and to see the positive in life. If you are the friend, help that person to see new reasons for getting up each day. Since loneliness usually makes depression and suicidal thoughts worse, spend a lot of time with friends and loved ones. Keep busy with activities. Seek medical attention. Many times suicidal behavior is a cause of a mental disorder, and professional help is therefore needed. A life may depend on it.

Also, pray and rely on the Lord so you can boldly declare, "I waited patiently for God to help me; then he listened and heard my cry. He lifted me out of the pit of despair, out from the bog and the mire, and set my feet on a hard, firm path, and steadied me as I walked along. He has given me a new song to sing, of praises to our God. Now many will hear of the glorious things he did for me, and stand in awe before the Lord, and put their trust in him" (Psalm 40:1-3 TLB).

Most importantly, choose life, for the Lord said, "'I call heaven and earth to witness against you that today I have set before you life or death, blessing or curse. Oh, that you would choose life…! Choose to love the

Lord your God and to obey him and to cling to him, for he is your life and the length of your days'" (Deuteronomy 30:19-20 TLB).

And remember, "Christ in you brings hope for all the good things to come" (Colossians 1:27 NLV).

Watch TESTIMONY–SUICIDE Video Clip

PREPARING FOR THE FINISH LINE – Invitation

If you feel weighed down by the world and don't know how to get relief, there's hope for you and it's found in Jesus Christ. He can give peace that surpasses all understanding to those who are His. If you would like to experience this hope and find rest in His arms, please repeat this prayer:

Lord Jesus, I thank You that You came to give life and to give it more abundantly.[3] I believe in my heart and confess with my mouth that You are the Son of God and that You died so that I could live.[4] Please forgive me for all of my sins. I know that You are alive and You have a plan for me so this day I choose life! Thank You, Jesus. In Christ's name I pray, Amen!

WORSHIP – Listen to the Song CAN'T CLIMB THIS MOUNTAIN

ENDURANCE – Closing Prayer

Heavenly Father, I thank You that I can find hope in You. Nothing is ever so hopeless that You can't rescue me. It is through Your loving-kindness that I was born again to a new life and have a hope that never dies. Right now I come against any lies of the enemy and I cover my mind with the blood of Jesus. Help me to take every thought captive and to think only about what is true and pure. Thank You, Jesus, for life. In Your mighty name I pray, Amen!

TIPS AND RESOURCES – SUICIDE

Memory Verse: For I know the plans I have for you, declares the Lord, plans to prosper you and not to harm you, plans to give you hope and a future (Jeremiah 29:11).

If you or someone you know is contemplating suicide:

1. Pray.
2. Immediate intervention is crucial.
3. Talk to someone who can help you find other options and to see the positive in life.
4. If it's your friend, help that person to see new reasons for getting up each day.
5. Since loneliness usually makes depression and suicidal thoughts worse, spend lots of time with friends and loved ones.
6. Keep busy with activities.
7. Seek professional help.
8. Choose life!

Help Lines:

1-800-SUICIDE	24-Hour Hotline
1-877-332-7333	Real Help for Teens Hotline
1-877-727-4747	Suicide Prevention Line

Links:

www.christianliferesources.com/article/suicide
www.walking-wounded.net
www.sprc.org/settings/faith-based
www.christiancounselingcoalition.org
www.suicidepreventioncenter.org
http://teenlineonline.org/talk-now/#sthash.nJ0EHzfF.dpuf

Sword of the Spirit:

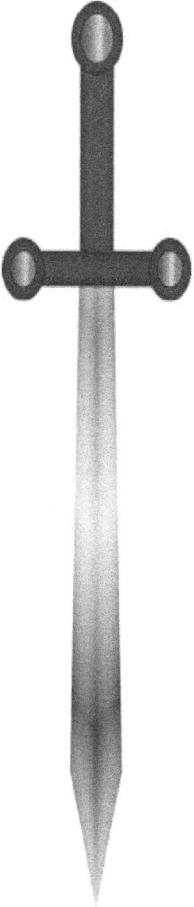

Why am I so sad? Why am I so upset? I tell myself, "Wait for God's help! You will again be able to praise him, your God, the one who will save you" (Psalm 42:11).

I waited patiently for God to help me; then he listened and heard my cry. He lifted me out of the pit of despair, out from the bog and the mire, and set my feet on a hard, firm path, and steadied me as I walked along (Psalm 40:1-4 TLB).

Oh, that you would choose life..! Choose to love the Lord your God and to obey him and to cling to him, for he is your life and the length of your days (Deuteronomy 30:19-20 TLB).

Christ in you brings hope of all the great things to come (Colossians 1:27 NLV).

We wait in hope for the LORD; he is our help and our shield. In him our hearts rejoice, for we trust in his holy name. May your unfailing love be with us, LORD, even as we put our hope in you (Psalm 33:20-22 NIV).

Witnessing

WITNESSING

Bible References Romans 10:14, 1:16; Mark 16:15, 6:3; Jeremiah 1:6–8; Acts 9:10–19; 1 Corinthians 2:3, 12:3; John 4:37, 6:44; 1 Peter 3:15–16; Jonah 1:1–4, 1:17, 2:10, 3:4; Matthew 5:16

> **Memory Verse:** But before people can pray to the Lord for help, they must believe in him. And before they can believe in the Lord, they must hear about him. And for anyone to hear about the Lord, someone must tell them (Romans 10:14).

Opening Prayer – Lord, through Your Word teach me, challenge me, guide me and equip me, Amen!

Watch WITNESSING–Lesson Video Clip

SETTING THE PACE – Your Thoughts and Experiences/ Discussion Group

1. Have you ever had an opportunity to share Christ with someone but didn't because you were afraid to? If so, how did that make you feel?

2. Have you ever shared your faith with someone, and if so, what was that experience like?

3. What are some excuses that people use for not sharing their faith?

4. What are some ways that you can share Jesus with others?

RUNNING THE RACE – Study

In the movie, *Steadfast*, two Christian teenage sisters handle sharing their faith in different ways. Lydia fails to share Jesus with her best friend for fear that it would hurt their friendship, and when Jesse dies she suffers from tremendous guilt that Jesse might not have felt the need to take his own life if he had only known the hope of Jesus Christ.

Moriah, on the other hand, makes her life a living testimony. She treats others with kindness even when they don't deserve it, and she also has the boldness to tell people about Jesus. Through the way she handles situations, she wins Claire to Christ. Claire sees a peace in Moriah that she doesn't have and she is drawn to it. In this same manner, we can draw others to Christ also. Our lives may be the only Bible someone else reads and our actions may be what draws them to Jesus.

Winning others to Christ isn't only about sharing scripture and telling people about Jesus. Witnessing begins with how you live your own life. Put into practice five W's and an H of Christian living: Watch **who** you hang around with; be careful of **what** you say and do; **when** life is tough, stay calm and in prayer; be mindful of **where** you go, and **how** you dress and treat others. Live a life of integrity. In this way, when others see you acting differently than the rest of the world, then you can share the **why**.

Romans 10:14 states: "But before people can pray to the Lord for help, they must believe in him. And before they can believe in the Lord, they must hear about him. And for anyone to hear about the Lord, someone must tell them." We are called to be that someone.

Jesus said, "Go everywhere in the world. Tell the Good News to everyone" (Mark 16:15). Yet most of us are fearful of this commission, partly because we are too focused on ourselves. We are afraid of rejection, fearful we will offend someone, scared to lose a friendship, and anxious that we won't know the answer to something. Yet while we are protecting ourselves, others are perishing with no hope. We are to be "proud of the Good News, because it is the power God uses to save everyone who believes" (Romans 1:16).

You might think, "I don't know what to say—I'm just a teen." In

Jeremiah Chapter 1, Jeremiah had those same doubts when the Lord told him to witness:

> [Jeremiah] replied, "I'm not a good speaker, LORD, and I'm too young."
>
> "Don't say you're too young," the Lord answered. "If I tell you to go and speak to someone, then go! And when I tell you what to say, don't leave out a word! I promise to be with you and keep you safe, so don't be afraid." (1:6-8 CEV)

Even though God promises to be with us and to keep us safe, another excuse Christians use for not witnessing is that they are fearful of what others might say or do to them if they share Christ. In the book of Acts, there was a disciple named Ananias who was called by God to go to someone who had been putting Christians into prison and even having them murdered. Ananias had every right to be scared, but the Lord sent him anyway:

> In Damascus there was a disciple named Ananias. The Lord called to him in a vision, "Ananias!"
>
> "Yes, Lord," he answered.
>
> The Lord told him, "Go to the house of Judas on Straight Street and ask for a man from Tarsus named Saul, for he is praying. In a vision he has seen a man named Ananias come and place his hands on him to restore his sight."
>
> "Lord," Ananias answered, "I have heard many reports about this man and all the harm he has done to your holy people in Jerusalem. And he has come here with authority from the chief priests to arrest all who call on your name."
>
> But the Lord said to Ananias, "Go! This man is my

chosen instrument to proclaim my name to the Gentiles and their kings and to the people of Israel. I will show him how much he must suffer for my name."

Then Ananias went to the house and entered it. Placing his hands on Saul, he said, "Brother Saul, the Lord—Jesus, who appeared to you on the road as you were coming here—has sent me so that you may see again and be filled with the Holy Spirit." Immediately, something like scales fell from Saul's eyes, and he could see again. He got up and was baptized, and after taking some food, he regained his strength. (Acts 9:10-19 NIV)

After this event, Saul's name was changed to Paul and he became one of the most influential disciples and even wrote most of the New Testament. What if Ananias had refused to go?

Yet even Paul, like Ananias, struggled with fear at times when witnessing. The Bible says that when Paul went to speak to the church in Corinth, he came "in weakness with great fear and trembling" (1 Corinthians 2:3 NIV). But even though he was afraid, he still spoke of Christ. We are to have that same obedience.

Jonah was a prophet in the Bible who was not obedient to God's calling. When God told him to witness to the people of Ninevah, Jonah didn't want to:

The LORD spoke to Jonah son of Amittai: "Nineveh is a big city. I have heard about the many evil things the people are doing there. So go there and tell them to stop doing such evil things."

But Jonah tried to run away from the LORD. He went to Joppa and found a boat that was going to the faraway city of Tarshish. Jonah paid money for the trip and went on the boat. He wanted to travel with the people on this boat to Tarshish and run away from the LORD.

> But the LORD brought a great storm on the sea. The
> wind made the sea very rough. The storm was very strong,
> and the boat was ready to break apart. (Jonah 1:1-4)

Jonah explained to the frightened sailors that the storm was because of him. So the men threw Jonah into the sea:

> When Jonah fell into the sea, the Lord chose a very
> big fish to swallow Jonah. He was in the stomach of the
> fish for three days and three nights. (Jonah 1:17)

Jonah finally prayed to God and promised to do as He asked:

> Then the LORD spoke to the fish, and it vomited
> Jonah out of its stomach onto the dry land. (Jonah 2:10)

Through the story of Jonah we learn a lesson about the consequences of disobedience, but we also discover another important truth. When Jonah finally went to the city of Ninevah, his message from the Lord consisted of only a few words. He told the people, "After forty days, Nineveh will be destroyed!" (Jonah 3:4). It was nothing eloquent or even heartfelt because Jonah still didn't really want them saved, but the people of Nineveh believed God and repented of their sins. Jonah didn't have to deliver a long message with all the right scriptures. The people believed because God spoke to their hearts.

Salvation is the Lord's job. We must remember that while we are to be obedient and pass out the invitations, it is the Holy Spirit who must bring each person to the party. Just as we are not to worry about what to say because the Lord will speak through us, we mustn't take it personally if people don't immediately accept the message. People are saved by the power of God, not us. 1 Corinthians 12:3 states: "No one can say, 'Jesus is Lord,' without the help of the Holy Spirit." Also, John 6:44 points out: "No one can come to me unless the Father who sent me draws them" (NIV). People will only be saved through being convicted of their sins by the Holy Spirit and by being willing to repent.

Again, as vital as we know His message to be, not everyone will receive it and that doesn't mean it's due to our delivery. Many didn't listen even when it was Jesus Himself speaking it. In fact, He faced rejection especially from those closest to Him. While teaching in his own hometown, "they were deeply offended and refused to believe in him" (Mark 6:3 NLT). Yet Jesus continued His ministry.

Don't allow yourself to become discouraged and stop witnessing if you don't personally experience someone accepting Christ. The Bible says, "One person plants, but another person harvests the crop" (John 4:37). It may be that God is using you to plant the seed while someone else might witness the act of salvation.

While salvation is not up to us, giving the opportunity is. People are drowning in their sins and it is up to us to throw them a lifeline, while the ultimate decision to grab that lifeline is theirs. God has an appointed time to work in a person's life. We are to be in continual prayer so that the Lord will lead us to the people who are ready for His Word. The Lord led Philip to just the right person in the Book of Acts:

> An angel of the Lord spoke to Philip. The angel said, "Get ready and go south on the road that leads down to Gaza from Jerusalem—the road that goes through the desert."
>
> So Philip got ready and went. On the road he saw a man from Ethiopia. He was a eunuch and an important official in the service of Candace, the queen of the Ethiopians. He was responsible for taking care of all her money. This man had gone to Jerusalem to worship. Now he was on his way home. He was sitting in his chariot reading from the book of Isaiah the prophet.
>
> The Spirit said to Philip, "Go to that chariot and stay near it." So he went toward the chariot, and he heard the man reading from Isaiah the prophet. Philip asked him,

"Do you understand what you are reading?"

The man answered, "How can I understand? I need someone to explain it to me." Then he invited Philip to climb in and sit with him. (8:26-31)

The official began asking Philip questions, and Philip started there and then continued to share with the man the Good News about Jesus. The official accepted it and afterwards was baptized in a body of water nearby.

The Lord may not speak to us aloud anymore like with Philip, but He speaks to our hearts and through His Word, and He will direct us to opportunities, just like he did with Philip. Prayer is essential. Being in constant communion with the Lord and having a right relationship with Him prepares us to share His Word with others. Just as we enjoy telling our friends all about our boyfriend or girlfriend, our sacred romance with the Lord and our love for Christ should burn in us so strongly that we can't wait to share Him with others. Our passion will fuel the desire and the Spirit will guide our actions. The Bible says:

But keep the Lord Christ holy in your hearts. Always be ready to answer everyone who asks you to explain about the hope you have. But answer them in a gentle way with respect. Keep your conscience clear. Then people will see the good way you live as followers of Christ, and those who say bad things about you will be ashamed of what they said. (1 Peter 3:15-16)

Someone once asked Charles Spurgeon, one of the greatest preachers of all time, how he defends the Bible. "Very easy," he responded. "The same way I defend a lion. I simply let it out of its cage." Let's go forth now and roar like a lion!

Watch TESTIMONY–WITNESSING Video Clip

PREPARING FOR THE FINISH LINE – Invitation

You can't be an effective witness unless you have personally experienced the saving grace of Christ. If you have never completely surrendered your life to Jesus, now is your chance. Please repeat this prayer:

Lord Jesus, I ask You to forgive me for the ways I've sinned and for not living my life for You. I believe that You are the One True God who was crucified for me but is alive today. Thank You, Jesus, that I can now walk in the boldness of Christ, that the Holy Spirit will guide me, and that Your love for me is so strong that it just pours out of me onto others. Thank You, Jesus, for winning my soul. Amen!

WORSHIP – Listen to the Song *IT IS FOR JESUS*

ENDURANCE – Closing Prayer

Heavenly Father, help me to have the boldness to go into the world and proclaim the gospel to everyone. Let my light shine before others so that they may see my good works and give glory to my Father who is in heaven.[1] Give me the courage to not be ashamed of the gospel, for it is the power of God for salvation to everyone who believes.[2] Prepare the hearts and minds of those You would have me to witness to so that they will come to the saving knowledge of Jesus Christ. As at Pentecost, fill me with the power of Your Holy Spirit. Let me go forth now and be a soul winner for You. In Jesus' name I pray, Amen!

RESOURCES – WITNESSING

Memory Verse: But before people can pray to the Lord for help, they must believe in him. And before they can believe in the Lord, they must hear about him. And for anyone to hear about the Lord, someone must tell them (Romans 10:14).

Links:

www.christianwitnessingtools.com
http://peacewithgod.net—The gospel shared through videos, testimonies and scriptures. Great site to share with others.
www.creativebiblestudy.com/how-to-witness.html—Tips on how to share your faith and free Christian tracts to download.
www.fervr.net—An award-winning Christian youth site with free teen devotions, movie reviews & videos.
www.OneWish4U.com—effective method of evangelizing; resources

Sword of the Spirit:

But keep the Lord Christ holy in your hearts. Always be ready to answer everyone who asks you to explain about the hope you have. But answer them in a gentle way with respect. Keep your conscience clear. Then people will see the good way you live as followers of Christ, and those who say bad things about you will be ashamed of what they said (1 Peter 3:15-16).

Go everywhere in the world. Tell the Good News to everyone (Mark 16:15).

WAYS TO EVANGELIZE

Since every person and situation is unique, a different approach to evangelizing may be required for each circumstance. Prayer is foremost in having the boldness of Spirit and the wisdom to use the most acceptable approach. Always be prayed up. Remember we are to love people into the Kingdom instead of trying to argue them there. Following is a basic guideline to evangelizing:

1. Model the example of Jesus when He witnessed to the woman at the well:

    a. Try to speak to the person alone, if possible. People tend to respond better that way.

    b. Start with small talk, then turn the conversation to Christ by asking something like, "Do you go to church?" The answer to that question will impact what you say next. Some people attend church but don't have a relationship with Jesus, so it's important to establish that fact. An engaging question to ask is: "If you could wish one thing from God today for you, what would that be?" This is non-threatening and causes people to speak from the heart. (Taken from www.OneWish4U.com—visit this valuable website for more indepth information, lessons, and tools for witnessing to others.)

2. Depending on the situation, it may be inspiring to share your testimony and what the Lord has done for you. Ahead of time write out your testimony so you will be prepared.

3. For an easy-to-follow visual way to share the gospel, the wristband from *One Wish* is highly effective.

4. Also a combination of scripture found in Romans and also the Ten Commandments can be used to witness. Ask:

    a. *Do you consider yourself a good person?* Well, Romans 3:10 says: "There is no one doing what is right, not even one."

    b. *We all need salvation because we've all sinned.* Romans 3:23 confirms: "All have sinned and are not good enough to share God's divine greatness."

    c. If you don't believe you're a sinner, let's look at God's law–the Ten Commandments:

        1. Put God first
        2. Worship only God
        3. Use God's name with respect
        4. Remember God's Sabbath
        5. Respect your parents

6. Don't murder (having anger in your heart is the same)
7. Don't commit adultery (looking at someone with lust is the same)
8. Don't steal
9. Don't lie
10. Don't envy others.

d. *Stealing one little thing, telling a little white lie, or even holding onto anger makes you a sinner.* James 2:10 says: "You might follow all of God's law. But if you fail to obey only one command, you are guilty of breaking all the commands in that law."

e. *What is the price of sin?* Romans 6:23 tells us: "When people sin, they earn what sin pays—death. But God gives his people a free gift—eternal life in Christ Jesus our Lord." Just as a good judge wouldn't let the guilty go free, we too must be punished for our sins.

f. *But instead someone else took our punishment–Jesus Christ died for our sins.* Romans 5:8 says: "But God showed how much he loved us by having Christ die for us, even though we were sinful" (CEV).

g. *Just how are we saved?* Romans 10:9-10 tells us: "So you will be saved, if you honestly say, "Jesus is Lord," and if you believe with all your heart that God raised him from death. God will accept you and save you, if you truly believe this and tell it to others" (CEV).

h. *The assurance of our salvation comes from Romans 10:13:* "All who call out to the Lord will be saved" (CEV).

5. *Make Jesus the Lord of Your Life and Grow in Your Faith:* Pray daily and read the Bible (the Gospel of John is a good place to start); put God first; go to church weekly; love others and share Jesus with them.

ABC Salvation Prayer:

Lord, I **admit** that I am a sinner, but I **believe** You died on the cross for my sins and to give me eternal life. I **confess** my sins and ask You to come into my heart, wash it clean, and help me to live for You. In Jesus' name I pray, Amen!

I have fought the good fight.
I have finished the race.
I have served the Lord faithfully.

2 Timothy 4:7

Sample Answers for Setting the Pace

Bullying:

1. What are some examples of bullying?

   (Answers may consist of: physical—hitting, spitting, biting, punching, scratching; emotional—name calling, threatening, spreading rumors, telling others not to be friends with someone, leaving someone out on purpose; cyber-bullying—using electronic technology such as texts, social media, chat, blot, websites)

5. What do you believe make some people targets for bullying?

   (Answers may consist of: appearance; social status; race; religion; the way they act)

6. Why do you believe some people become bullies?

   (Answers may consist of: poor social skills; been bullied themselves-possibly at home; crave power; lack of compassion for others; wants others to think he/she is tough; low self-esteem; too much self-esteem)

Purity:

1. Why should we remain pure when everyone else seems to be "doing it?"

   (Answers may include: just because everyone else is supposedly doing it doesn't make it right; we are to live holy lives; God's Word tells us that we are to wait until marriage; we are to remain pure so we can get the full blessing of God on our relationship; our first time can't be re-gifted; that is something special for our future husband/wife)

2. What are some consequences for not remaining pure?

   (Answers may include: unwanted pregnancy; sexually transmitted diseases; forced marriage; married too young; broken relationship with God; unable to share that part of you with your true soul mate)

3. What could girls and guys do to help each other stay committed to purity?

(Answers may include: dress more modestly; never be alone in a house together; set boundaries together; be careful of what you watch; pray together; don't allow yourselves to get in tempting situations; respect each other)

Eating Disorders:

2. The media hypes thinness. How do you think this feeds into eating disorders?

(Answers may include: it gives the impression that to be successful and happy, one has to be thin and look a certain way)

6. Name some eating disorders.

(Answers may include: bulimia; anorexia; binge eating; exercise bulimia)

7. What are some signs of an eating disorder?

(Answers may include: weight gain; weight loss; skipping meals; using the bathroom right after eating; avoiding eating around others; taking laxatives; excessive exercise; wearing baggy clothing; obsession over food and/or looks)

8. Why do you think some people develop eating disorders?

(Answers may include: low self-esteem; perfectionism; anxiety disorders; family problems; sports or other activities; peer pressure; bullying)

12. Is it true that people with eating disorders are always underweight?

(Answer is no—many ED sufferers are of average weight and even overweight)

13. How can sports play a part in eating disorders?

(Answers may include: many sports focus on weight)

14. What are some problems that eating disorders can cause?

(Answers may include: heart problems; low blood pressure; dehydration; fatigue; muscle loss; dry brittle bones; hair loss; dry skin and hair; growth of hair all over the body; tooth decay; rupture of esophagus; peptic ulcers; kidney and gallbladder problems)

15. Can eating disorders cause death?

(Answer: yes—among other things, it can cause organ and heart failure. Anorexia has the highest death rate of any mental illness)

Substance Abuse:

1. What are some reasons teens drink and do drugs?

    (Answers may include: escape; self-medication; peer pressure; boredom; rebellion; lack of confidence; experimentation; social acceptance; depression; family or relationship problems; problems in school)

2. Name some different types of drugs.

    (Answers may include: alcohol; marijuana; cocaine; crack cocaine; PCP; LSD; crystal meth; speed; mushrooms; inhalants; heroine; prescription drugs)

4. What are some ways to avoid getting involved in drugs, smoking and/or alcohol?

    (Answers may include: be careful of who you hang out with; keep busy with positive activities; be aware of the consequences and health risks; don't think that you won't get addicted; make up in your mind you won't do drugs, drink alcohol or smoke cigarettes)

5. What kind of wrong decisions could possibly be made while under the influence of drugs or alcohol?

    (Answers may include: driving drunk or high and injuring or killing someone else or even yourself; getting involved in other illegal activities, getting arrested; becoming sexually active and suffering from sexual diseases, unwanted pregnancy; getting into fights)

6. What influences around you might contribute to drug use, alcohol consumption or smoking?

(Answers may include: peer pressure—wanting to fit in; going to parties where these activities are going on; wanting to be like famous people who are engaging in these activities)

7. What are some effects of marijuana?

(Answers may include: drowsiness; dry mouth; bloodshot eyes; increased hunger; impaired short-term memory, coordination, and concentration; paranoia; increased heart rate; lower sperm count in men; increased risk of infertility with women)

Cutting:

1. What is self-injury and what types are there?

(Answers may include: intentionally inflicting harm on oneself by cutting, burning (with cigarettes, etc.), hair pulling, head banging, scratching, pinching)

2. What areas of the body are most common for cutting?

(Answers may include: arms, wrists, legs, thighs, stomach)

3. Why do you think people self-injure?

(Answers may include: self-punishment; relieve frustration; distraction from problems; express pain; to try to gain a sense of control; to feel again)

4. What are some things that might trigger self-injury?

(Answers may include: family problems; relationship issues; bullying; stress; sexual abuse; parents divorcing; school or job problems)

5. List activities that can help a person calm down.

(Answers may include: pray; read the Bible; listen to music; take a bubble bath; talk to a friend; journal; draw; exercise; play with a pet)

6. True or false: Everyone who cuts is suicidal.

    (Answer is false. Those who are suicidal want to end all feelings but self-injurers want to feel better)

7. True or false: People who cut are seeking attention.

    (Answer is false. Cutters tend to keep it a secret and are ashamed)

8. If you found out one of your friends was cutting, what would you say to him or her?

    (Answers may include: stay calm and not act shocked; be compassionate; ask what is bothering the person; listen intently but non-judgmentally; suggest seeking help from an authority figure and offer to go with her or him, avoid making the person feel guilty)

Abuse:

1. Why do you think some people are abusive?

    (Answers may include: problems with drugs or alcohol; they were abused themselves; anger management issues; mental health issues; stress)

2. Do you think anyone who abuses others is ever justified?

    (Answer is no)

3. Do you think that those who have been abused will become abusers? If so, why?

    (Answers may include: yes, they often do. They are taught to believe that abuse is okay and the abuser is the one who gets what he/she wants; they don't learn empathy for others)

4. Why do you think that so many victims of abuse keep quiet about it?

    (Answers may include: fear; shame; unwarranted guilt; humiliation; feel the need to protect the abuser)

5. What are some ways a victim might escape an abusive situation?

(Answers may include: seek help—confide in someone you trust, such as a pastor, teacher, parent or the authorities; don't argue with a drunk or drugged abuser; coordinate a backup plan—have a safe place to go, store emergency numbers on your phone)

6. What would you say to someone you know who is being abused, either physically, sexually or emotionally? How might you help them?

   (Answers may include: support her/him; listen nonjudgmentally; help your friend understand it's not her/his fault; encourage the person to seek professional help)

7. In what ways was Jesus abused?

   (Answers may include: He was betrayed; beaten; whipped; spit on; hung on a cross to die; people shouted insults at him)

Suicide:

1. Why do you think people decide life isn't worth living anymore?

   (Answers may include: troubles at school; failed relationships; bullying; stress; problems at home; pressure to succeed; fears of failure; physical or mental abuse; no hope; death in family; depression)

3. If you think someone you know is considering suicide, should you tell someone?

   (Answer: yes, threats of suicide should be taken seriously)

4. What can you do to help a friend who is talking about suicide?

   (Answers may include: pray; share the hope of Christ; listen; encourage medical attention; be positive and uplifting; help the person to see that God has a great plan for their future and think of things for your friend to look forward to; get her or him to talk to a trusted adult)

Witnessing:

3. What are some excuses that people use for not sharing their faith?

   (Answers may include: afraid of what others will think; someone might make fun of me; someone might get mad at me/beat me up; afraid to lose someone's friendship; afraid someone will ask me a question I don't know the answer to)

4. What are some ways that you can share Jesus with others?

   (Answers may include: invite them to church; give them tracts or books; personal testimony; wear clothing with scripture; acts of kindness; by example)

NOTES

BULLYING

1.   Sewell, Dan, Julie Carr Smyth, and Andrew Welsh-Huggins. "1 Killed, 4 Wounded In School Shooting At Chardon High School - CBS Cleveland." CBS Cleveland. CBS Radio, Inc., 27 Feb. 2012. Web. 21 June 2014.

2.   Pearson, Holly Yan. Michael, Michelle Hall, Steve Almasy, Matt Smith, Jason Hanna, Stephanie Elam, Evan Perez, Amanda Watts, Chuck Johnston, and Kim Segal. "Nevada School Shooting 911 Call: 'I Got a Kid down Who's Been Shot'" CNN. Cable News Network, 01 Jan. 1970. Web. 21 June 2014.

3.   Woda, Tim. "Girl, 12, Jumped to Death After 18 Months of Cyberbullying." Girl, 12, Jumped to Death After 18 Months of Cyberbullying. UKnow.com, 12 Sept. 2013. Web. 10 Aug. 2014.

4.   Sit, Ryan, and Rocco Parascandola. "Girl, 15, Jumps to Death off Grandma's Upper West Side Apartment Building." NY Daily News. New York Daily News, 13 Feb. 2014. Web. 10 Aug. 2014

5.   "11 Facts About Bullying." DoSomething.org. DoSomething.org, n.d. Web. 09 Aug. 2014.

6.   Romans 10:9 (paraphrased)

BULLYING AND THE BYSTANDER

1.   Atlien. "Twitter Fail: Teen Sent 144 Tweets Before Committing Suicide & No One Helped..." Straight From The A [SFTA]. N.p., 11 Nov. 2011. Web. 10 Aug. 2014.

2.   Livingston, Ikimulisa. "Stabbed Hero Dies as More than 20 People Stroll past Him." New York Post Stabbed Hero Dies as More than 20 People Stroll Pasthim Comments. New York Post, 24 Apr. 2010. Web. 10 Aug. 2014.

3.   "Police: As Many as 20 Present at Gang Rape outside School Dance." CNN. Cable News Network, 28 Oct. 2009. Web. 10 Aug. 2014.

4.   "Education Site." Bullying Statistics. The Family Resource Facilitation Program, 2014. Web. 10 Aug. 2014.

5.   Whitson, Signe. "6 Reasons Why Bystanders Choose Not to Intervene to Stop Bullying." The Huffington Post. TheHuffingtonPost.com, 19 Nov. 2013. Web. 10 Aug. 2014.

6.   Romans 10:9 (paraphrased)

7.   John 13:34 (paraphrased)

8.   John 15:13 (MSG, paraphrased)

PURITY

1. Romans 10:9 (paraphrased)
2. Deuteronomy 6:18 (NIV)
3. 2 Corinthians 5:17 (CEV)
4. Psalm 51:10 (NIV)

EATING DISORDERS

1. "Eating Disorders." US News. U.S.News & World Report, 2010. Web. 10 Aug. 2014.
2. "The Eating Disorder Foundation." The Eating Disorder Foundation. The Eating Disorder Foundation, 2013. Web. 10 Aug. 2014.
3. "'Girls' Star Zosia Mamet Opens up on Her Struggle with an Eating Disorder." Fox News. FOX News Network, 12 Aug. 2014. Web. 12 Aug. 2014.
4. Vujicic, Nick. "About Nick: His Story." Attitude Is Altitude RSS2. Attitude Is Altitude, 2013. Web. 10 Aug. 2014.
5. Segal, Jeanne, PhD, and Melinda Smith, MA. "Eating Disorder Treatment and Recovery.": Help for Anorexia and Bulimia. N.p., 2014. Web. 09 Aug. 2014.
6. Psalm 138:8 (NKJV)
7. Jeremiah 31:3

SUBSTANCE ABUSE

1. "MADD - Mothers Against Drunk Driving." MADD - Mothers Against Drunk Driving. Mothers Against Drunk Driving, 2014. Web. 21 June 2014.
2. "Indy Week." Indy Week. Indy Week, 2014. Web. 21 June 2014.
3. Unger, Todd, Marcus Moore, and Ryan Wood. "Alcohol Suspected in Wreck That Killed Good Samaritans." WFAA Wfaa.com. WFAA, 16 June 2013. Web. 11 Aug. 2014.
4. Greenhill, Sam. "Teen Died of Drugs Overdose as Friends Listened on Skype."Mail Online. Associated Newspapers, 16 Nov. 2013. Web. 11 Aug. 2014.
5. Bern, Gesellschaftsstrasse 78 3012. PK 40-25648-4 - IBAN No.: CH97 0900 0000 4002 5648 4 Www.ifbc.info Alcohol and Drug Use: Know the Facts (n.d.): n. pag. Alcohol and Drug Use: Know the Facts. International Blue Cross, 2011. Web.
6. "11 Facts About Teens And Alcohol." DoSomething.org. N.p., n.d. Web. 11 Aug. 2014.
7. Edwards, Ashton. "Teen Drug Overdose Deaths Surpass Car Accident Deaths in U.S." KFORcom. KFOR-TV, 30 Aug. 2013. Web. 11

Aug. 2014.

    8. "Youth and Tobacco Use." Centers for Disease Control and Prevention. Centers for Disease Control and Prevention, 14 Feb. 2014. Web. 10 Aug. 2014.

    9. "Prevent Teen Drug Use: Research." Prevent Teen Drug Use: Research. N.p., n.d. Web. 11 Aug. 2014.

    10. "Jim's Story." PBS. PBS, n.d. Web. 22 June 2014.

    11. Hebrews 12:1

    12. Romans 10:9 (paraphrased)

CUTTING

    1. "Cutting Statistics and Self-Injury Treatment - Teen Health." Cutting Statistics and Self-Injury Treatment - Teen Health. Teen Help, 2014. Web. 11 Aug. 2014.

    2. Romans 10:9 (paraphrased)

    3. Romans 8:38-39

    4. Isaiah 53:5 (NIV)

ABUSE

    1. "National Child Abuse Statistics." Prevention and Treatment of Child Abuse. Childhelp, n.d. Web. 10 Aug. 2014.

    2, "Child Abuse in America." Child Abuse in America. Tennyson Center for Children, n.d. Web. 10 Aug. 2014.

    3. "11 Facts About Child Abuse." 11 Facts About Child Abuse. N.p.,n.d.Web. 23 May 2015.

    4. Romans 10:9 (paraphrased)

    5. Deuteronomy 31:6 (paraphrased)

SUICIDE

    1. Brent, David, MD. "NAMI - The National Alliance on Mental Illness." NAMI. NAMI, n.d. Web. 12 Aug. 2014.

    2. "Angie Fenimore's Suicide Near-Death Experience." Angie Fenimore's Suicide Near-Death Experience. Kevin Williams, 2014. Web. 13 May 2015.

    3. John 10:10

    4. Romans 10:9 (paraphrased)

WITNESSING

    1. Matthew 5:16 (paraphrased)

    2. Romans 1:16 (paraphrased)

ABOUT THE AUTHOR

Barbara Shoner earned a master's degree in Theology, bachelor's degree in Biblical Studies, associate of science degree in Paralegal Studies, and certification with the American Association of Christian Counselors. She is passionate about missions, community outreach, and sharing the love of Jesus. Barbara is the screenwriter and producer of the feature film, *Steadfast*, which has also been awarded The Dove Foundation's Faith-Based and Family Friendly Ages 12+ Seals of Approval. More information can be found at: www.steadfastthemovie.com.

Her new release, *Umbrella in the Storm*, encourages readers to ride out the storms of life while learning to dance in the rain. To find out more, please visit: *www.barbarashoner.com*.

Barbara has joyfully survived the teen years and is enjoying the next season with her three children: two nearby in Florida and one who followed the Lord's calling to Japan. It's all about loving, laughing, and appreciating life.

OTHER WORKS
Steadfast the Movie
Steadfast the Movie Original Soundtrack
Steadfast the Movie Resource Video
Steadfast Teens
Steadfast Teens Devotional and Prayer Journal
Steadfast Parents Devotional and Prayer Journal
Umbrella in the Storm
"Attack of Minimalism" story published in *Chicken Soup for the Soul, Age is Just a Number*

REVIEW

Thank you for reading and participating in the Steadfast Study Guide. A review from you would be greatly appreciated. The Lord bless you and keep you.

Review on Amazon: **www.amazon.com/dp/B084LMF735**

We want to hear from you. Feel free to contact us with any comments, praise reports or prayer requests at: **steadfastmovie@gmail.com**

or visit our website at: **www.steadfastthemovie.com**

You will keep in perfect peace
those whose minds are steadfast,
because they trust in you.

Isaiah 26:3 NIV

www.ingramcontent.com/pod-product-compliance
Lightning Source LLC
Chambersburg PA
CBHW020547030426
42337CB00013B/995